This edition is published by:
BooksEast
29 Nelson Street
Deal
Kent
CT14 6DR

ISBN 978-1-3999-4302-4

© **Andrew Sargent 2023**

All rights reserved. No part of this publication may be reproduced, stored in a retrieval system, and transmitted in any way and by any means, electronic, mechanical, photocopying, recording or otherwise, without the prior written permission of the copyright holders.

The author has asserted his moral right.

A CIP catalogue record for this book is available from the British Library.

Edited and designed by Anita Luckett
Printed and bound by Precision Proto Group

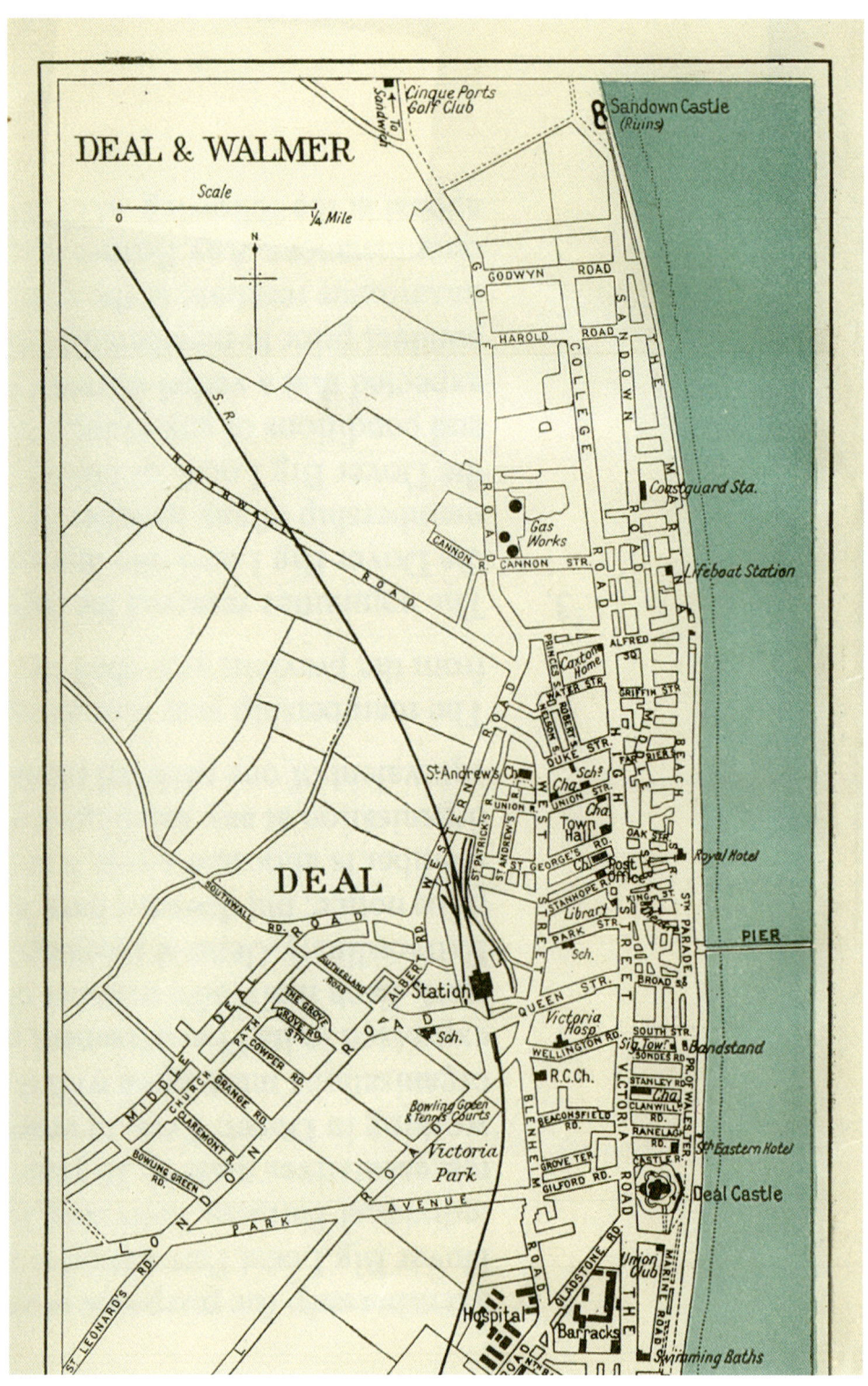

Taken from "A Pictorial and Descriptive Guide to Deal and Walmer" (1928 - 1929).

Contents

    Introduction   5

People
1. Frederick Browne, organ builder   6
2. Edward Hugessen Knatchbull-Hugessen, MP   9
3. Susannah Marsh and others, publicans   13
4. The Matthews family, Walmer brewers   15
5. George Mercer, Town Clerk   18
6. Sir Henry Rushbury, drypoint engraver   21
7. Revd Henry Venn, Rector of Walmer   25

Objects
8. Seventeenth century Deal trade tokens   28
9. When Deal used its own banknotes   31
10. Mrs Kennett's spirit flask   36
11. Lemonade, ginger beer and "Zolakone" bottles   40
12. Stylish advertising c.1903   43

Leisure
13. Seafront entertainment at the Pavilion   47
14. The Independent Order of Oddfellows   50
15. Rounders, quoits and trap-bat at the Castle Inn   52
16. A remarkable discovery at the Lord Clyde   54
17. The Rose Hotel, High Street (with Steve Glover)   57
18. The Swan Hotel, Queen Street (with Steve Glover)   61

Society
19. A staggeringly corrupt by-election   65
20. The Cinque Ports Artillery Volunteers   69
21. Civil Defence in 1940   73
22. Sandwich Prison 1829 - 1879   77
23. "Refractory seamen" withdraw their labour   81
24. Cheating boatmen   85
25. The tragedy of the Pride of the Sea   88

    Index   91

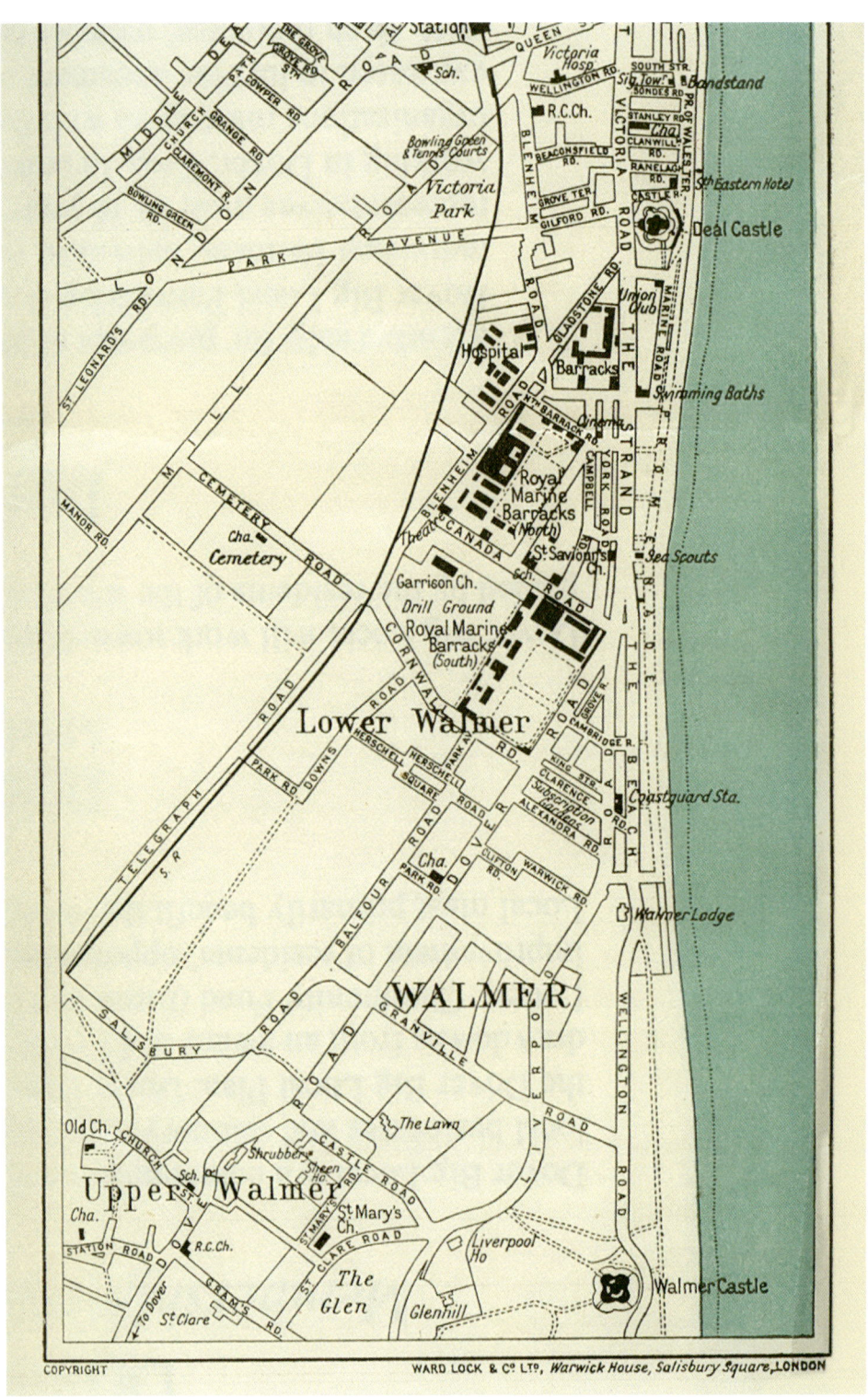

The boundary between Deal and Walmer runs through Deal Castle.

INTRODUCTION

The first edition of the Deal, Walmer and Sandwich Mercury (Downs Reporter and Cinque Ports Messenger) appeared in 1865. The paper has been published continuously ever since, and is now the Deal and Sandwich edition of the East Kent Mercury.

The paper has a valuable tradition of publishing articles on the history of Deal, Walmer, Sandwich and the surrounding area. Many different authors have helped to sustain the Mercury's history pages over the years.

The twenty five articles in this collection appeared between 2016 and 2019, initially under the strap line of "Those Were the Days" and then, from 2017, of "Mercury Memories".

Although not obvious from the title of this collection, several of the articles look beyond Deal and Walmer to make connections with the neighbouring town of Sandwich.

The articles are reproduced here as they were written, save for a few minor corrections. Almost all of the images are those used at the time, though the captions have sometimes been adjusted.

April 2023

1.

Frederick Browne, organ builder

Few people passing through the village of Ash will guess that, inside an old school building, a marvellous new musical instrument is being completed – a new church pipe organ, no less.

It will soon be installed in the Roman Catholic church of St John the Evangelist, Mongeham, and will be blessed at a special service on 21 September at 6.00pm.

There will be a second reason to celebrate. The company building the instrument, F H Browne & Sons, began life in 1871 in Deal and over the next 35 years built organs there for most churches in the town and for many others in Kent and beyond.

How wonderful that the tradition continues to this day.

Frederick Browne must have been a remarkable young man. At the age of 22, after an apprenticeship in Canterbury, he started his own business in a redundant Baptist chapel in Nelson Street, Deal.

Across the country churches and chapels were eagerly equipping themselves with impressive new organs, and Frederick's skills and enterprise quickly bore fruit.

F H Browne's music shop in Deal High Street.

By the 1880s his Kent Organ Works had an excellent reputation, and was winning prestige commissions like the enlargement of the great organ at Rochester Cathedral.

Often several organs were being built at the same time. Indeed a national register lists almost 70 organs built by F H Browne for churches in the UK between 1871 and 1906.

Almost every church in Deal and Walmer invested in a sizeable F H Browne organ. The new organ for St Mary's Walmer, for example, unveiled in 1888, had 1,354 pipes and "an entirely new pneumatic system of Mr F H Browne's devising", the tubing for which, if laid end to end, would reach "very nearly a mile and a quarter".

To meet burgeoning demand, Browne increased capacity by building a large new workshop between Nelson Street and West Street. On the ground floor was the metal and machine shop, and above that the carpenters' shop. Organs were assembled in the former chapel building.

Repair work and tuning also provided steady income, and in the 1880s the company opened a music shop in Deal High Street selling keyboard instruments and sheet music.

F H Browne also enjoyed success overseas, building organs for churches in France, Canada, Egypt and elsewhere, and opening an office in Calais. In the 1890s it offered to tune instruments "in any part of the country and on the Continent".

Frederick and his wife Eliza had six children, two of whom followed him into the business. They owned several properties in Deal in addition to the organ works, and Frederick served as churchwarden at the nearby St Andrew's parish church.

Frederick Browne (front right) and family.

But in 1904 the company very nearly hit the buffers. An expensive lawsuit in connection with an organ built for a church in Vancouver, persistent late payments and the practice of allowing extended credit combined to force the company into voluntary liquidation.

Frederick and his sons had to sell most of their assets in Deal, including their High Street shop. In February 1905 came the auction of timber and machinery from the organ works, and later that month the property itself was put up for auction.

Yet F H Browne survived. New premises were rented in Canterbury and the company continued to build, repair and tune organs. Frederick Browne and his son William steered the company until their deaths in the 1930s.

In 1983 the firm moved from Canterbury to Ash. Plans are now in hand to relocate to a purpose-built workshop in East Stourmouth. So the company will remain in east Kent.

Today F H Browne & Sons (Organ Builders) tunes and maintains over 600 instruments as well as building bespoke pipe organs. The new organ for St John the Evangelist – a "tracker" organ with 2 manuals and 17 stops – is the first large organ of this type that the company has built for 100 years.

An F H Browne organ made in Deal recently enjoyed a surprising new lease of life. Earlier this year the organ in the former Deal Baptist Church in Victoria Road, now home to the Community Church Deal, was generously donated to a church in Mazères in south-west France.

The congregation there are thrilled with their organ, fully restored and making wonderful music once again.

F H Browne's shop at 42 High Street was bought by Goulden and Wind and continued as a music shop until 1980.

The workshop Frederick built for his Kent Organ Works still stands, and the old Baptist Chapel, where he constructed so many fine organs, is now a family home.

Nelson Hall, as it is now known, will be open to visitors on 15 September as part of the Deal and Walmer Heritage Open Days programme.

The F H Browne organ in the former Deal Baptist church.

"Organ making firm survived hard times", published on 19 September 2018.

2.

Edward Hugessen Knatchbull-Hugessen, MP

For 50 years after the 1832 Reform Act Deal was part of the parliamentary borough of Sandwich. There were not many electors – only 2,115 on the register in 1880 – but there were two MPs: Sandwich was a "double member" constituency.

The MP who co-represented the borough between 1857 and 1880 had a great door-stop of a name: Edward Hugessen Knatchbull-Hugessen. Edward – as he had better be for the rest of this article – was not only a career politician for many years but was an avid book collector, an author and the editor of the letters of one of the country's most celebrated novelists.

Edward's father was Sir Edward Knatchbull, an "Ultra-Tory" Kentish grandee. But he himself was elected as a Liberal, and his maiden speech in the House of Commons in 1858 was made in support of the abolition of church rates.

The following year Palmerston appointed him a junior whip, and he subsequently served as a junior minister under Prime Ministers Russell and Gladstone.

For a time he was a rising star in the Liberal Party. But he does not seem to have been very popular, and was never given a Cabinet post. One modern historian refers to him dismissively as "jealous and ambitious".

Edward used this picture for a visiting card in the 1860s.

Edward did not live in the constituency – this is a more modern expectation – but was a regular guest of honour at dinners and celebrations in Deal and Sandwich.

The opening of Deal's new iron pier in 1863.

In April 1863, for example, Edward drove in the first pile of Deal's new iron pier amidst great fanfare and rejoicing. He returned in November the following year to perform the final opening ceremony.

Both as an opposition MP and as a junior minister Edward took care to maintain close links with national representatives of brewers and licensed victuallers. Many in the Liberal Party were becoming converts to the temperance cause but Edward had little sympathy.

He found himself in a difficult position after 1868 when serving under a Home Secretary determined to crack down on the number of public houses. Edward manoeuvred skilfully, or shamefully according to the teetotal lobby, and no doubt was relieved to be moved to the Colonial Office in 1871.

Edward was fortunate that from 1868 his fellow Liberal MP for the borough was Henry Brassey, second son of the railway contractor Thomas Brassey. Extremely rich, he spent large sums in the constituency and some of his resulting popularity clearly rubbed off on his colleague.

In 1880, soon after being re-elected – the Conservatives did not think it worth fielding a candidate – Edward accepted a peerage and entered the House of Lords as the first Lord Brabourne.

Rather ungratefully, one might have thought, he then joined the Conservatives. Two years later he helped to form the Liberty and Property Defence League to promote the free market and oppose "grandmotherly legislation".

His resignation as an MP had precipitated a scandalously corrupt by-election. The constituency was ignominiously disenfranchised, and abolished in 1885 when Deal and Sandwich disappeared within the new much larger constituency of St Augustine's.

The new peer kept himself busy both in politics and as a writer. A wonderful opportunity to make his mark in the literary world came from the fact that his mother Fanny, the daughter of Edward Austen Knight of Godmersham Park near Ashford, had been one of Jane Austen's nieces (and allegedly her favourite).

When Fanny died in 1882 Edward inherited 94 of his great-aunt's letters to her elder sister Cassandra. He edited and published these in two volumes in 1884.

His introductory comments on Jane's letters, alas, were subsequently described in the Dictionary of National Biography (DNB) as being "mainly notable for their diffuse irrelevance".

A cruel caricature in Vanity Fair, June 1870.

But he had yet another string to his bow – as a writer of children's stories. Introducing his first volume he explained that most "were originally told to my children in the pleasant half-hours before the arrival of their bedtime and the sound of the dressing-bell interrupted our evening talk".

His stories have not really stood the test of time. Although the DNB grudgingly admits that they were "sometimes attractive" it also quotes the judgement of two experts in children's literature that Edward's stories were also "often long-winded, macabre and sadistic".

To be fair, tastes in children's literature have changed a great deal since the days of

Jane Austen, as sketched by her sister Cassandra.

Hans Christian Andersen, whom Edward said had been his model.

On the brighter side, one of his early tales is said to have been admired by J R R Tolkein and to have provided some inspiration in creating characters for the Lord of the Rings.

Edward remained an important figure in the affairs of the county. He was for many years chairman of the East Kent Quarter Sessions – the county magistrates – and was also deputy chairman of the South-Eastern Railway. He lived in Smeeth, a village south-east of Ashford, dying there in 1893 aged 63.

Edward's eldest son was briefly Liberal MP for Rochester and his grandson Michael, a Conservative, represented Ashford for a time in the 1930s.

Two holders of the Baronetcy were killed whilst serving with

Ernest and the Toad, from "Stories for My Children" (1869).

the Grenadier Guards. The 3rd Baron, a highly regarded ornithologist, was killed in France in 1915. Norton, the 6th Baron, was wounded and taken prisoner in Italy in 1943 and then executed by the SS after an unsuccessful escape attempt.

The 7th Baron, John Knatchbull, Edward's great-grandson, married the elder daughter of Earl Mountbatten of Burma. A film producer who received two Academy Award nominations, he served as Pro-Chancellor of the University of Kent and, for over 40 years, as a governor of Wye Agricultural College.

Tragedy struck the family when his mother and one of his twin sons were killed alongside his father-in-law in 1979 when the IRA blew up Mountbatten's motorboat in Donegal Bay. He and his wife were seriously injured but recovered. John died in 2005 at the age of 80.

"MP, author and county statesman", published on 27 October 2017.

3.

Susannah Marsh and others, publicans

In late Victorian times women were not often found drinking beer in Deal's public houses and beerhouses. But many spent long hours on the other side of the bar, managing the house and its sometimes unruly customers in their husband's absence.

This was particularly the case when the publican was also a boatman, at sea or busy on the beach, or when he plied a second trade as a carpenter or decorator and left his wife, and perhaps a daughter or two, to serve the beer and keep order.

The magistrates did not usually grant licences to women in their own right. But there was a major exception to the rule. If a married male publican died in harness his widow was almost always allowed to take on the licence.

Some women then attempted to keep the business going under their own steam but came to grief – like Emma Gunner, who ran the Brickmaker's Arms off-licence on Mill Road after her husband died but was prosecuted several times for serving on the premises and called it a day.

But there were many examples of women who remained in charge for many years and enjoyed success and a very good reputation.

The "highly respected" Alice Allen, for example, ran the Royal Hotel after her husband died in 1871 until her own death seven years later. Charlotte Donoghue, another widow, ran the Royal Exchange and when she died her daughter took over.

Probably the two most renowned women licensees were Susannah Marsh of the Admiral Keppel and Amelia Kemp of the Yarmouth Packet.

Susannah ran the Admiral Keppel in Upper Deal between 1864, when her husband James died, and 1902. For many years she hosted lavish annual dinners to celebrate the election of the (entirely unofficial) "Mayor of Upper Deal".

Sarah Licence, wife of the landlord of the Saracen's Head.

Susannah Marsh ran the Admiral Keppel (left, middle distance).

Amelia Kemp had been married to the landlord of the Crown, which then stood north of the Royal Hotel. Her husband was a violent drunkard, and in 1874 her daughter – very bravely – enlisted the help of the magistrates. Perhaps in sympathy, her husband having quit the scene, they allowed Amelia to take the licence of another Beach Street house, the Yarmouth Packet.

This was an inspired decision. "Mrs Kemp's Yarmouth Packet" became a celebrated North Deal establishment, particularly favoured by Trinity House pilots in need of lodgings.

A second category of lodgers who stayed at the Yarmouth Packet were French labourers employed at the nearby canning factories. Amelia took good care of them, and nursed them in times of illness. In 1907, after the death of one of the workers, the Mercury reported that she had sent a wreath and organised a subscription for his family.

"Mrs Kemp's Yarmouth Packet" painted by John Lewis Roget in 1888.

Amelia remained in charge until 1908. The Yarmouth Packet closed on 31 December 1919. The Admiral Keppel, renamed the Farrier, still serves the people of Upper Deal.

"Wives stepped into publicans' shoes", published on 11 August 2016.

4.

The Matthews family, Walmer brewers

The discovery of a large painted advertisement for Thompson & Son of Walmer on the front of The Lighthouse (reported by the Mercury on 13 June) is a reminder of days when this local brewery owned the majority of pubs in Walmer and Deal.

The Walmer Brewery was owned by the Matthews family for over 80 years until sold to Charringtons in 1951. On 20 June the Mercury published a fascinating picture – shown here again – of the whole Matthews family.

Who were the nine people gazing out at us from in front of the Old House, their family home in Walmer?

The picture was probably taken around 1885. It belongs to Chris Hicks, co-owner of The Rose in Deal High Street. Chris is a great-grandson of John Matthews. In the picture John can be seen sporting a bushy white beard and holding on his knee his youngest son George – Chris's grandfather.

John Matthews (seated) and family.

John Matthews had begun his career as a brewer in London. In 1853 he married Mary Thompson, and in 1867 purchased the brewery from her brother Morris and settled in Walmer. Matthews energised the business, modernising the brewery and buying more public houses, but retained the name Thompson & Son.

Seated next to him is his second wife Jessie, and clustered around are their young children – from left to right John, Dorothy, Jessie, George and Richard.

Behind stand Willie (left) and Arthur Matthews, John's sons from his first marriage. The elder brother, Arthur, had practised as a barrister after education at Harrow and Oxford but returned to Walmer to join the family business. Willie lived at the Old House, opposite the brewery, Arthur nearby at the Shrubbery.

Willie Matthews and his wife were talented amateur musicians, he on the cello and she on the violin. In the picture of the interior of the Old House (shown here, with thanks again to Chris Hicks) can be seen a violin and a baby grand piano.

Musical instruments on display in the Old House.

Willie was involved in running the brewery but Arthur seems to have carried the main load after their father died in 1895. In 1901 the company bought Hills brewery in Deal, and with it another 63 pubs and beerhouses.

In the 1920s, the son of the head brewer later recalled, "the whole of Upper Walmer was influenced by the brewery. The smell of beer pervaded the whole area and its tall chimneys were visible for miles... the brewery never closed, although work stopped on the whistle".

Arthur combined his business responsibilities with membership of Walmer Council, which he chaired for sixteen years, service as a magistrate and active involvement in a formidable number of causes.

These included following in his father's footsteps as a leading figure within the Deal and Walmer Conservative and Unionist Association. According to one former employee "whenever there was a General Election the brewery was decorated with local Conservative Party colours… whatever your opinion, no one dare oppose the Matthews".

Both brothers owned large, chauffeur driven cars. In November 1908 the Mercury reported that Willie's car had accidentally knocked down James Laming, coxswain of the Kingsdown lifeboat, who had been "walking with a box of herrings on his shoulder along Church-street". Laming suffered bruises and abrasions but lived to tell the tale.

Two of the five young children in the family picture, one smiling cheerfully and the other looking rather nonplussed, are dressed in sailor suits. It is sobering to realise that both would be killed in the First World War.

John, on the left, fought in the Boer War with the Northumberland Fusiliers but was killed in September 1914, aged 35, at the Battle of Aisne. Richard was killed almost exactly three years later when serving in France with the West Yorkshire Regiment.

Their sister Jessie lost her husband on active service in 1916. They had married, the bride in a "blue moiré velours and hat of blue with blue ostrich feathers", only a few weeks before war was declared.

Arthur had married Constance Townsend, the daughter of a Vice Admiral, in 1897. They had one daughter, Eileen. A picture in Deal Library shows her dressed as Britannia at the 1919 Peace Pageant held in the grounds of Walmer Castle.

Sadly Eileen pre-deceased her parents, dying in 1934 aged 36. Arthur and Constance dedicated new choir stalls in St Mary's church to her memory.

Eileen Matthews as Britannia in 1919.

Arthur himself, still a director of Thompson & Son, died two years later at the age of 77. He had been, said the Mercury, "held in the highest esteem… respected not only for his reputation as a man, but also for ever-readiness to befriend those in need".

The Old House, in front of which John Matthews, his seven children and his wife Jessie had posed all those years before, was demolished in the 1960s. In due course Thompson Close took its place.

The brewery buildings, derelict for many years, were finally pulled down in 1981.

"Days when brewery dominated town", published on 1 August 2018.

5.

George Mercer, Town Clerk

In April 1890 a special ceremony was held at Deal Town Hall. In the presence of members of the Council the Mayor of Deal presented the Town Clerk, George Mercer, with an illuminated address to mark almost 50 years of public service.

A public subscription had raised £100, the intention being to commission an oil painting of Mr Mercer to hang in the Town Hall. But he had generously asked that the money should instead be donated to Mary Hougham's almshouses.

The 71 year-old Mercer was in fact a very worried man. His business affairs were in a mess, and eighteen months later his life would end in tragedy and public humiliation.

George Mercer was born in 1819, the son of the solicitor and banker John Mercer. In due course he became a partner in his father's firm, and when John died in 1844 George succeeded him as coroner and as Clerk to the Deal Magistrates.

Over time Mercer secured almost every local public office to which a solicitor could aspire. These included serving as Clerk to the Deal Pavement Commission for almost 50 years and then as Town Clerk, and as Clerk to the Walmer Local Board for 26 years.

His offices in Queen Street also served as the offices of the Cinque Ports Magistrates – for whom, almost inevitably, he acted as Clerk.

Mercer's business partner was his brother-in-law James Barber Edwards. Their work included investing and dispersing large sums of money from endowments, estates and bequests.

The Queen Street offices once used by Mercer & Edwards.

By the early 1880s Mercer was a man under pressure. Edwards had been out of action for six months serving hard labour for corrupt practices during the 1880 by-election, and in 1882 Mercer complained bitterly to him about his "great carelessness, great neglect for years, and utter confusion in a great many of your transactions".

Edwards, for his part, would have little hesitation when the time came in blaming Mercer for most of the firm's problems.

In 1887 Mercer and Edwards took as a third partner John James Williamson. The firm may already have been insolvent and the young Williamson, who invested £2,250, felt himself thoroughly misled. In June 1891 he succeeded in dissolving the partnership, and struck out on his own.

The demise of Mercer & Edwards was precipitated by a petition that September to the Canterbury Bankruptcy Court claiming that Mercer had suspended payments and that Edwards had fled the town.

George Mercer's family were now very worried about his mental state, and tried to keep knives and razors out of his reach. But on 5 October, after breakfasting in bed at his house in Victoria Road, Mercer shot himself through the heart with a silver-plated pistol he had recently bought in London.

Over the previous fortnight creditors had been withdrawing their deeds and available securities as fast as they could, and now the town was "thrown into the greatest consternation".

The state of affairs at Mercer & Edwards was worse than anyone could have imagined. Accounts in the ledgers were "extraordinarily confused" and rarely accurate, but the Official Receiver finally arrived at figures of £87,146 for the firm's liabilities against assets of only £18,074.

James Barber Edwards lived in this handsome High Street house.

Business had been conducted shambolically for decades. No cash accounts had been kept since 1861, and annual balance sheets had been abandoned as a waste of effort. Profits and losses were a mystery.

For Mercer & Edwards' clients the distress caused by the bankruptcy "has unfortunately been widespread, many… having all their property in the firm's hands".

This was not just the result of woeful mismanagement. The following year James Barber Edwards, aged 76, pleaded guilty to charges of fraud. He was sentenced to eight years penal servitude and packed off to Lewes Gaol.

George Mercer's last home was in Victoria Road.

Against the odds, Edwards survived his second term of imprisonment. He was then given a home in Southborough by two unmarried daughters and died in 1911 at the ripe old age of 93.

George Mercer had long since been quietly interred in Deal Cemetery. The flag on the Town Hall was flown at half mast, and "a number of the tradesmen partially closed their establishments". His wife Susanna Mercer was left destitute, and her husband's funeral fees of £16.13s had to be met by the Official Receiver. She died two years later.

John Williamson, who had wisely extracted himself from the partnership before disaster struck, replaced Mercer as Clerk to the Deal Magistrates, and built a successful legal practice.

His wife's nephew Reginald Barnes joined him as a partner in 1934, and the firm of Williamson & Barnes continues to this day in the Queen Street offices once occupied by Mercer & Edwards.

"Town clerk died after public humiliation", published on 11 July 2018.

6.

Sir Henry Rushbury, drypoint engraver

One chilly day, not long before the First World War, a young artist was observed making sketches of a brick kiln on the outskirts of Sandwich. His name was Henry "Harry" Rushbury. To his sister he wrote:

"I go to my Rembrandt spot and there stand on one leg in a cold wind; drawing with a flock of sheep and Sandwich's dirtiest children looking on".

Rushbury was born in Birmingham in 1889 and initially trained as a designer of stained glass. Having moved to London in 1912 he learned the skills of etching and drypoint (a technique involving scratching lines into a polished copper plate).

Rushbury's reputation would be built on his mastery of these techniques. But he also developed into an accomplished water-colourist.

Henry Rushbury in 1914.

His drypoint print of the Sandwich brick kiln was published in 1914. It shows a rather imposing collection of buildings which dwarf the carts and workmen gathered around. A moored sailing barge is partially visible.

We do not know what drew the young man to the Sandwich area. But he would make at least two more prints of the town. The first – "The Brewery, Sandwich" – was also completed in 1914 and was exhibited at the Royal Academy the following year. In 1916 came "Sandwich Haven", which shows a brewer's dray heading slowly along the quay.

Rushbury's brewery print is particularly striking. At the centre rises the tower of the East Kent Brewery Company, with the masts of vessels moored in the Stour showing alongside.

But the picture is not strictly "true to life". Rushbury has drawn on different sketches and impressions of the town to create a satisfying work of art.

Rushbury exhibited his print of "The Brewery, Sandwich" at the Royal Academy in 1915.

In 1916, although medically classified as C3 ("Sedentary Service at Home Camps"), he was conscripted to the East Surrey Regiment. From there he transferred to the Royal Flying Corps and in 1918 became an official War Artist with the rank of second lieutenant.

After the war Rushbury resumed his career as a professional artist. He spent at lot of time on the Continent, and many of his prints show scenes in France and Italy. In 1920, however, he published a print entitled "Old Deal". This was based on drawings made several years before.

Most artists visiting Deal over the years have been drawn inexorably to the seafront. But not Rushbury. Instead he chose to depict a boatbuilders' yard some distance from the beach. But, like his picture of the Sandwich brewery, it is a composite image – an artistic interpretation combining different images, perspectives and imagined details.

It seems as if the starting point for the picture was the view looking east up Wellington Road towards South Street. To the left several men are completing work on a new lugger. Others stand above on an overhanging balcony. Planks cover the ground, and a woman and child are just visible standing at the stern of the boat.

This is indeed more or less where Hayward's boatbuilding yard had once stood. Thomas Hayward and his son Isaac had between them run the business for 100 years. The luggers they built were hauled up South Street to the beach on greased wooden planks.

But Isaac had died in 1887 and by the time of Rushbury's visit the yard had long since closed. The artist must have been told about it, or perhaps had seen an old photograph, and his imagination was sparked.

Rushbury took many other artistic liberties in the cause of creating an interesting and pleasing image. He often chose to depict imposing and monumental structures and here, from a low vantage point, buildings rise solid and high on either side of the street, reaching to the top of the print.
A vague impression of South Street can be seen in the distance and so too – although not in reality visible from this vantage point – is the Timeball Tower.

This splendid evocation of "Old Deal" was exhibited in 1920.

One can imagine Rushbury stolling around the town sketching scenes and details that caught his eye – the balcony on the left, for instance, looks a little like the one which then projected seawards from the rear of the Fountain public house on Beach Street.

This was still standing when Rushbury made his sketches but was demolished two years after the print was published and exhibited at the Royal Academy.

The third "state" (ie version) of the Deal print, illustrated here, incorporated a horse and cart in the middle distance and two tie beams connecting houses on either side of the street.

Rushbury's "Brick Kiln, Sandwich" dates from 1914.

Rushbury does not seem to have returned to East Kent subject matter, and from 1930 made his home in Suffolk. By then the flourishing American market for British etchings and drypoints had been undermined by the effects of the Wall Street crash.

Rushbury became a Royal Academy Associate Academician in 1927, and a full member in 1936. During the Second World War he again served as a War Artist.

In 1949 Rushbury was elected Keeper of the Royal Academy Schools, a post he held until 1964. Under his watch the reputation of the schools rose once again to equal those of the RCA and the Slade.

His eminence within the art establishment was rewarded with a Knighthood in 1964. He died in 1968 aged 78.

Rushbury was described in later life as "a small humorous figure with a rubicund countenance, sharp blue eyes, white hair and side whiskers" and, according to the painter Sir Alfred Munnings, "could charm a bird off a tree".

Sir Henry Rushbury RA had come a long way from the days when he was observed by locals "standing on one leg" sketching on the outskirts of Sandwich.

"Artist's satisfying views of the town", published on 4 October 2017.

7.

Revd Henry Venn, Rector of Walmer

It is March 1905 and the Vicar of St Mary's Walmer, Revd Canon Henry Venn, is feeling grumpy.

A special commission has just recommended against creating a separate parish for Lower Walmer. Canon Venn must continue to have charge of the parish church of St Mary's, Walmer Old Church and St Saviour's "chapel of ease".

He promises his flock that he "will under no circumstances again raise the question". But the decision rankles. Indeed Canon Venn is rarely slow to express disappointment, whether about an unsatisfactory response to an appeal for funds or the use of unsightly jam pots and pickle jars as receptacles for flowers placed on gravestones.

St Mary's Church, Walmer.

Yet his parish seems to be flourishing. St Saviour's is often full to bursting. In 1907 all 600 seats in St Mary's are taken for a choir concert (though alas the offertory raises only £5, £2 of which comes in coppers).

Twenty "District Visitors" help to keep in touch with parishioners, and the calendar is packed with lectures, outings and sales of work.

John Lewis Roget's picture shows St Saviour's on the right.

Among the many church groups are the St Saviour's Men's Society, the Upper Walmer Band of Hope, and the St Saviour's Dorcas Sewing Society which in December 1907 "distributes 125 warm and useful garments, principally amongst the very aged poor".

To Canon Venn's great relief the saga of the new burial ground finally comes to an end. Negotiations had begun as long ago as 1900 for the acquisition from the Leith Estate of a small plot of land next to the church.

There is a last minute problem. George Leith has already made it a condition that the bell of the Old Church may no longer be tolled for deaths and funerals. Now he wants to have it removed altogether.

Hurrah – the Vicar stands his ground and wins! The plot is conveyed to him, and in March 1906 new fencing is ordered.

Across the country dark clouds threaten. In particular the Church of England is terrified that the election of a Liberal Government in 1906 will open the way to a further attack on church schools.

Two years later the Vicar gives his views on the new Licensing Bill. He has been an abstainer since 1880 and "except when ill, or when travelling in foreign countries" has not since touched strong drink.

But he cannot support a forced reduction in the number of pubs, prohibition or even the call for total Sunday Closing. He has studied and witnessed the effects of temperance legislation in other countries: his mind is made up.

In September 1906 Canon and Mrs Venn take a well-earned holiday. They travel to New York, where the Vicar officiates at the marriage of his son.

He notes widespread prejudice, writing to his parishioners that "all our American friends are surprised (I might say a little shocked) that we have had a negro clergyman to dine at the same table with us, and even to sleep in one of the spare rooms at the Vicarage".

The couple then travel to Jamaica and delight in the flora and fauna. And they have a miraculous escape. Finding Kingston too warm they move inland and so escape the terrible earthquake which devastates the capital on 14 January 1907 and kills more than 800 people.

Canon Venn crossed the Atlantic on the RMC Victorian.

But the Venns will soon have their own private tragedy to endure. The following year, on holiday in San Remo, they receive a telegram announcing that their son has died. He was only 38, and had been employed at the US Bureau of Commerce.

The Canon's time in Walmer is drawing to a close. In May 1908 he announces his retirement, but cannot help adding that he might have stayed longer if the parish had been divided.

His successor is Revd Norman Radcliffe, returning from five years in New Zealand. Let us hope that his new parishioners take to heart Canon Venn's final admonition: "Every Clergyman coming to a Parish has his own ideas as to how things ought to be done. These alterations, in whatever direction they may tend, will annoy some of you. Give him credit for meaning well, and give him also credit for acting with judgement and knowledge".

"Walmer vicar was against prohibition plan", published on 22 August 2018.

8.

Seventeenth century Deal trade tokens

The Royal Mint has done its best to whip up interest in the new £1 coin introduced on 28 March. This twelve-sided, bimetallic coin incorporates a latent image, micro-lettering and "a high security feature built in to protect it from counterfeiting".

We usually take the coins we use every day for granted. We may dislike particular designs, and some of us still wistfully recall the noble half-crown or the elegant sixpence from pre-decimal days. But we assume there will always be coins available to buy small items or to receive in change.

This was not always the case. On several occasions the shortage of small denomination "coins of the realm" forced shopkeepers in Deal and in many other places to find an alternative way of enabling their customers to make purchases.

John Pittock's farthing token (above) and Ann Cauterel's 1669 token.

This occurred most dramatically between 1650 and 1674. During this period the governments of the Commonwealth and of King Charles II, preoccupied and impoverished, simply failed to mint any new copper coinage. The shortage of farthings and halfpennies in circulation became acute.

So, up and down the country, individual merchants and shopkeepers took the initiative and minted farthing or halfpenny "tokens" of their own. These were then used in their local areas as if they were actual currency.

Tokens were issued in at least 100 towns and villages in Kent. There were over 600 types, more than in any other English county. In Deal 18 different traders – grocers and bakers, drapers and chandlers – minted tokens between 1653 and 1669.

Tokens usually showed on one side the issuer's name and a coat of arms or design to indicate their trade, and on the other the place of origin and the issuer's initials, sometimes combined with those of their spouse.

Thomas Brothers from Deal, who was perhaps a grocer, chose a pair of scales for his token and William Coulson, more obscurely, an eagle and child. Peter Underwood, on the other hand, could not have been clearer: his design was a man making candles. Tokens had not only a practical purpose but were also an excellent early form of advertising.

It is interesting to note that almost 30 Kent tokens were minted by women. One such was Ann Cauterel of Deal, who in 1669 issued a halfpenny showing a pair of scales.

How did these tokens work? When shopping in Deal you might perhaps buy a bolt of cloth from John Lobdell with a silver coin and receive some of his tokens as change. The baker Moses Potter would then accept one or more of these tokens as payment for a loaf of bread, and give in change one of his own farthing tokens.

Peter Underwood, round the corner, would probably be quite happy to accept a mixture of these tokens when you bought

John Pittock and Ann Cauterel's tokens alongside a modern five pence piece.

some of his candles. After all that hard work you might be prompted to take some refreshment at the Dolphin alehouse in Lower Street having found one of their tokens in your purse; landlord Thomas Fitch would have been happy to oblige.

So round and round went the Deal tokens. But almost certainly only in Deal itself. Every so often a trader would probably swop tokens with other shopkeepers to replenish the supply of his own tokens.

Among those issuing tokens were both John and William Pittock. They would surely have been proud to know that generations of Pittocks would follow in their shoes as drapers and outfitters for over 200 years.

In 1959 the "Outfitter" magazine speculated that John Pittock of Deal might well be the country's "oldest business in the men's trade".

Charles II's government eventually got its act together. In 1672 the Royal Mint began again to issue farthings, with halfpennies following the next year. The minting of tokens became illegal and in December 1674 magistrates were told to take stern measures against offenders. Tokens disappeared from circulation, and if you later found some that you had squirrelled away or forgotten about – well, bad luck.

William Pittock's 1668 token showed a bust of James, Duke of York.

But the problem reappeared in the late eighteenth century. This time the scarcity of copper coins of the realm was felt particularly by manufacturers in the Midlands and North of England. Between 1787 and 1797 no less than 600 tons of copper were minted into tokens, with Birmingham the main centre of production.

So far as we know only one token was produced in Deal. This was a very handsome halfpenny token minted in 1794 by Richard Long, a Beach Street bookseller and stationer. Britain was now at war with Revolutionary France, and Long's token carried a powerful patriotic message – this was probably an important motivation for striking it. One side showed the arms of the Cinque Ports and the other a ship of the line in full sail with the legend "The Guard and Glory of Great Britain".

Tokens continued to circulate throughout the war. Finally the Government got a grip, and from January 1818 the minting of tokens (with some temporary local exceptions) became illegal once again.

But in Deal and Sandwich this was not the end of the story. Small purchases continued to be made without using British coin of the realm. If short of small change, never mind – French coins could be pressed into service instead! These were not of course tokens as such, but were used much as tokens had been used in previous centuries.

By the 1880s the use of French coins as penny and halfpenny tokens had become embarrassingly widespread in the maritime towns of Kent and Sussex. Among money-changers twelve French pennies (that is, twelve 10-centime pieces) were said be worth 11 ½d in British money.

Richard Long's halfpenny token.

The Government finally banned the import of foreign coinage in 1889, and not long afterwards bought up the estimated 8 million French coins in circulation at an exchange rate of 1 shilling for every 13 French "pennies".

In Deal the coins were bagged up at the post office and sent to the Royal Mint, though not before money-changers had made a tidy profit buying up coins at a poor rate of exchange before cashing them in. Henceforth anyone wanting to spend their French coins would have to cross the Channel to do so.

The saga of trade tokens in England, according to one historian, is "a story of the initiative of local authorities, companies and individuals in the face of state ineptitude". This may well be true, but it has also left behind very tangible evidence of the activities and enterprise of many local shopkeepers, merchants and innkeepers, both men and women.

"No small change? Shopkeepers in the town minted their own", published 5 April 2017.

9.

When Deal used its own banknotes

The new springy polymer £10 note entered circulation last week. The £5 note introduced last year had a mixed reception. Should we perhaps return to the time when Deal and Sandwich banks printed their own notes?

For over two hundred years small "country banks" provided much needed business credit and met a significant proportion of the nation's currency requirements. By 1812 there were more than 700 of these banks. Many printed their own notes. Strictly speaking these were "banker's cash notes". But they looked like bank notes, and were used and circulated locally in the same way as notes issued by the Bank of England.

The first bank in Deal known to have issued notes was founded by Thomas Oakley, merchant and brewer, in the early 1780s. It remained in business until his death in 1797.

Next to try their hand were a small group of partners (country banks could have no more than six) headed by the lawyer and former Mayor of Deal, John May. This opened in 1802 and during the boom years of the Napoleonic Wars the going was good. But the casualty rate among country banks was very high, particularly in the 1820s. May & Co's "Deal Bank" went bankrupt in 1825.

The third private bank, the Deal Commercial Bank, lasted the longest. Rather unusually it was founded by a doctor, William Hulke. Over the years his partners included the brewer John Iggulden, John Dixson (Hulke's son-in-law, another doctor) and Hulke's sons William and Benjamin. The bank opened in 1808 and for many years had offices at 22 Lower Street.

William Hulke senior, banker and doctor.

The younger William was also a doctor. But he first came to public notice when in 1816, aged 24, he was prosecuted for criminal conduct – that is to say, adultery – by Commodore Sir Edward Owen.

When Sir Edward applied to the House of Lords for a divorce the following year their Lordships heard evidence of improper intimacy between William and Lady Owen in Deal, and of adultery committed in Sandwich at the Bell Hotel.

The Deal Commercial Bank survived the scandal. But in 1840, having existed for over 30 years, it too went bankrupt. It was then absorbed by the National Provincial Bank, the first truly national bank in England. This in turn finally disappeared in 1970 after merging with the Westminster Bank.

The Hulkes' reputations do not seem to have suffered from the bankruptcy. Benjamin was town clerk for 22 years. His brother William achieved some fame for having given medical care to the young Princess Victoria at Walmer Castle in 1842, and ten years later for waiting on the ailing Duke of Wellington in his final days.

Sandwich's only country bank survived the Deal Commercial Bank by only a year but had lasted much longer. Founded in 1796, its partners over the years included brewers, surgeons and a grazier.

When the time came the partners were able to engineer a smooth exit. In 1841 the Sandwich Bank became a branch of the London and County Banking Company. The long-serving manager, Mr Reader, remained in charge, and all existing notes were honoured.

The death of the Duke of Wellington. William Hulke is on the left.

All four Deal and Sandwich banks designed and issued bank notes. Thomas Oakley's note was worth 5 guineas. The Deal Bank issued £1, £5 and £10 notes – for some reason it was only legal to print notes of under £5 between 1797 and 1826.

The proof for the design for a £5 note issued by the Deal Bank.

The specimen Deal Bank note, shown on page 32, has a version of the Cinque Ports coat of arms in a cartouche on the left and, harder to make out, "M W & Co" on the right. The "W" is probably May's long-term partner William Wyborn.

On display in the Deal Maritime and Local History Museum are several fragile £5 and £10 notes issued by the Deal Commercial Bank. They date from the 1830s and must have been collected and cancelled by the lawyers who handled the consequences of bankruptcy in 1840.

£10 notes issued by the Deal Commercial Bank in 1839.

Local banknotes often suffered a lot of damage (so perhaps there is something to be said for polymer after all). If sent through the post the sender might cut off the margins to save weight. It was also common to minimise risk by cutting a note in half and sending each part separately.

The loss of a note could be a very serious matter. In 1780 the Kentish Gazette carried the offer of a two guinea reward for the finder of a Deal bank note – presumably one of Mr Oakley's – lost between Canterbury and Birchington.

In 1809 disaster befell a traveller who contrived to lose two £10 Deal bank notes en route from Sholden to St Margaret's. In this case the reward offered was a whopping seven guineas.

Then there was the individual who managed to lose in Dover "forty-one pounds, in Deal Bank Notes, consisting of eight fives and a single one, inclosed in whited-brown paper". Let us hope some honest citizen did indeed find and return the package to the Three Compasses in Lower Street, as requested, and claim their well-deserved reward.

The Hulke family home in Lower Street.

Unluckier still was the man who in 1801 lost ("between Ramsgate and Sandwich, or at Sandwich") a red morocco pocket book containing £200, £125 of which were in Sandwich bank notes. In this case twenty guineas were offered in reward and the numbers of the notes were circulated in the hope that they would not be successfully cashed.

And of course notes might be stolen. In 1804 the proprietor of Walmer Court was beaten up by three soldiers and robbed of 14 £5 notes and a gold watch. One of his attackers was later transported to Australia after turning King's Evidence, and the others were sentenced to death.

Advertisements can give an valuable insight into the mix of notes a wealthy man might carry. A pocket book lost in 1810, presumably by a Sandwich resident, contained £28 in Sandwich notes of various denominations, two notes from a Canterbury bank, one from a Margate bank and only one Bank of England note.

Despite wear and tear, theft and deliberate mutilation some banknotes remained in circulation for a very long time.

In 1863 there was consternation at the Walmer barracks when a cash box belonging to the 6th Depot Battalion was stolen. It is surprising to learn that - more than twenty years after the closure of the Deal Commercial Bank - among the losses was a very dirty £5 Deal bank note. The mess manager reported that it had been "badly joined, and I think had been cut twice".

Yet, even so, a Canterbury butcher accepted the stolen note in payment for some rump steaks, and gave change. He in turn used it to settle an account with another butcher, and again the note seems to have been accepted without quibble.

By now the number of country banks in England and Wales had fallen dramatically.
The future lay with the newer joint-stock banks and the large clearing banks.

One last Deal bank did make a brief appearance in the 1880s, though it did not issue banknotes. This was the Deal and Walmer Trading Bank ("every description of banking business transacted"). Its manager, William Carterfield, had previously run boys' schools in the town.

As Gillian Chiverton has recounted (Mercury 5 July) his new career came to an abrupt end. On Monday 2 April 1888 the people of Deal awoke to the news that Carterfield had absconded with the contents of the safe and was last heard of, "carrying a small black bag", hitching a ride to Dover with two members of the London Rifle Brigade.

A £100 reward was offered for information leading to his arrest. But it seems unlikely that the description given – "of gentlemanly appearance, medium height and dark complexion" – was much help, and the rogue presumably made good his escape to France.

His embezzlements amounted to £1,200. Some shareholders hoped that the bank could still be saved. But the Directors quickly appointed a liquidator to wind up its affairs and close its office in King Street.

So ended, rather ignominiously, the town's 100 year experience of local banking.

The National Provincial Bank (centre) had earlier absorbed the Deal Commercial Bank.

"When town banks issued their own notes", published on 20 September 2017.

10.

Mrs Kennett's spirit flask

Some years ago Pat and Rodney George, then living in the Norfolk village of Great Ryburgh, decided that the floor of their spare bedroom needed attention.

Up came the floorboards and there, amidst a century or more's accumulation of dirt and debris, lay an old stoneware bottle. It carried the roughly impressed words "A Kennett, Star Inn, Deal".

In due course Pat visited Deal to see if the Star still existed but could find no trace of it. She then contacted the Deal Society for help.

The spirit flask made for Ann Kennett in the 1830s.

The building that was once the Star Inn is still there, on the corner of Middle Street and Brewer Street. It began life as the Two Brewers, and in the eighteenth century was a venue for cock-fighting, among other pastimes. It became the Star around 1804.

But who was A Kennett? Alfred or Albert, perhaps. Not at all; "he" was a "she", and her name was Ann.

Ann Goodchild was born in 1791 and married William Kennett around 1810. They had at least seven children, all baptised in St George's church. In about 1820 William took the licence of the Star, and the family moved to their new home in Middle Street.

William died in 1829. Ann, then aged 38, had a choice: to let the licence of the Star pass to someone else, or to persuade the brewers and the magistrates to let her run the pub herself. She chose the second course. It was not unheard of for the widow of a landlord to take over the licence, but they did not often remain in charge for very long. In 1830 only five of Deal's 39 publicans were women.

Ann held the licence of the Star for some ten years. This gives an approximate date for the bottle. After 1842 the licence was held by one or other of her sons for several years, and Ann probably remained in the house.

The building in Norfolk where the flask was discovered.

The bottle is in fact a flask: that is, it was manufactured and used to contain spirits. As the holder of a full licence Ann was entitled to sell spirits as well as beer and wine, to drink on or off the premises.

The flask may have been filled and stoppered for immediate take-away. But it is more likely that the customer chose their drink – probably gin, brandy or whisky – and that Ann filled the flask, using a spirit measure, from a cask or barrel.

Few stoneware spirit flasks carrying the name of a Kent publican or wholesaler seem to have survived. This is in contrast to the many stoneware storage jars and ginger-beer bottles, manufactured over a much longer period, which can be found for sale and in collections.

Ann's flask is made of salt-glazed stoneware. The manufacturing process involved firing the clay to a very high temperature and then adding salt to the kiln. This made the vessel impermeable to water and gave it a characteristic finely pitted surface.

Flasks could also be partially dipped in a glaze before being fired, as in the case of Ann Kennett's order.

Firing the stoneware kilns was an exhausting and noxious business. The process produced hydrogen chloride gas and a great deal of dense white smoke. If mixed with water this would create hydrochloric acid.

It is almost certain that the flask was made in London. Stoneware flasks were manufactured there in large numbers between the 1820s and 1850s, though the main centre for stoneware production as a whole was Derbyshire.

The Dorset clay used to make Ann's flask would have been formed in a mould rather than thrown. By the mid-1830s flasks were generally cast in a flattened "ovate" form, with a flat base, to facilitate packaging and transport. We can be pretty sure that Ann's completed order would have been sent round by sea.

It's fair to say that her flask is not top of the range. The shoulder decoration is not particularity fine, and the lettering is crude. But it has survived!

The former Star Inn, having seen better days.

It would be fascinating to know which other Deal publicans invested in purpose-made spirit flasks. After all, the Star was not one of the larger pubs in Deal, and its competitors would have sold spirits too.

At present I know of only one other example. This was a flask commissioned in the 1840s by the landlord of the Swan on Queen Street. It was later owned by the brewers but has probably long since gone to ground.

Why did Mrs Kennett order a special batch of flasks? Was this a way of showing that the Star was still going strong despite her husband's death? Perhaps she rather enjoyed getting one-up on the male publicans running nearby pubs.

But the main reason must have been that selling spirits in a flask with her name on it, and that of the pub and the town, would increase the chance of empties finding their way back to her.

Clearly this did not always work! We will never know how a Deal spirit flask came to rest in a Norfolk village. But a good guess would be that a merchant seaman, ashore from a ship in the Downs, stocked up with a ration of spirits before making sail, and away went the flask.

The last of the Kennett publicans left the Star around 1848, and Ann moved to Erith. She died in 1855.

Her old pub began to acquire a dodgy reputation, with James Elson being accused of bringing a group of prostitutes with him when he moved from Ramsgate to take on the licence.

Elson mended his ways, and in 1876 transformed the Star into the Paragon Music Hall. It claimed to be "the only place in Deal to enjoy an evening's entertainment".

The final name change came in 1899 and it was as the Empire Theatre of Varieties that the house was finally closed by the brewers four years later.

The restored building is now a private residence.

Steve Glover and Michael Rogers record that the the building was later used as a leisure and reading room, a social and billiards club and a dairy before finally becoming a private house.

With many thanks to Pat George, and to Neil Smith for sharing his extensive knowledge of stoneware spirit flasks.

"Discovery of old flask led couple to Deal", published on 16 May 2018.

11.

Lemonade, ginger beer and "Zolakone" bottles

Feeling thirsty? How about a refreshing glass of Zolakone? Or a glass of "Crystal" potash water, very palatable and "useful in all Affections of the Kidneys". No? Then perhaps just some aerated mineral water or a bottle of ginger beer.

All these drinks, and many more besides, were manufactured in Victorian Deal and Walmer.

The market for soft drinks developed rapidly in the second half of the nineteenth century. By 1900 average annual consumption was around two gallons per head. A large proportion of these drinks was locally produced.

For grocers it could be a very useful sideline. Stephen Parker, an Upper Deal grocer, began brewing ginger beer in 1852. Edward Adams, grocer and toy dealer, followed suit at his premises in Lower Street three years later.

Parker and his son – the latter declared elected to the council in 1898 to cries of "good old ginger beer" – continued in the business for more than sixty years. Deliveries were made by a special ginger beer van.

High street chemists were sometimes tempted to try their hand. In Edwardian times these included, at 8 The Strand, the Walmer chemist Henry Wood ("Manufacturer of High Class Mineral Waters").

Not everyone stayed the course. In the 1860s William Browning traded as a ginger beer manufacturer at 185 Middle Street. But by 1869 he had tired of the business and taken the licence of the nearby Druid's Arms public house.

Significant capital investment might be needed. In 1860 the "manufactory" next to the Swan Hotel in West Street included
"a steam engine and boiler, soda water machine and cylinder and Tyler's Patent Bottling Machine", not to mention three "spring wagons", a dog cart and a pony.

As time went on entrepreneurs became more ambitious, but with mixed fortunes. The Dover mineral water manufacturer James Pratt chanced his arm in purchasing the West Street factory. But a fire in 1881 destroyed the stables, and Pratt went out of business the following year.

More successful was the Dover and Folkstone-based company Souter Mackenzie & Co, manufacturers of a range of "Crystal" mineral waters and cordials.

In 1900 they opened a small works in Deal High Street. Rather appropriately this was next to, or possibly in the yard of, the Victoria Temperance Hotel. The company made much of being army and admiralty contractors, and probably hoped to attract custom from the marine barracks. But they faced competition from a "Royal Marines Depot" manufacturer of mineral water and ginger beer, presumably located in or near the barracks themselves.

At the top of the tree was J W Court & Son of Walmer. The business was founded in 1879 and their factory in North Barrack Road modernised in 1886. This included installing the "celebrated "Porter Clark" process" to soften and purify the water.

A reporter from the Mercury found the factory "a perfect maze of pipes, travelling in all directions, bewildering to the uninitiated". But happily "by a few words from the manager, their uses are made tolerably clear".

The interior of J W Court's factory in North Barrack Road.

By 1900 Courts were producing "soda water, seltzer, potass, lithia, lemonade, ginger ale, zolakone, and the old-fashioned home-brewed ginger beer, for which latter, especially, an enormous demand exists".

Local companies did not have it all their own way. Manufacturers in other East Kent towns did their best to muscle in, sometimes sending their wagons on speculative runs. Philpott's of Ramsgate were especially persistent, occasionally arousing the anger of the town sergeant for blocking streets and avoiding tolls.

Some manufacturers aimed directly at temperance customers. How about, for instance, an invigorating glass of Hires Root Beer: The Great Temperance Drink, made from sixteen wild roots and berries?

J W Court in contrast lined up with the publicans, even at one point becoming chairman of the local Licensed Victuallers Association – a sign that pubs were themselves selling significant quantities of soft drinks.

Ginger beer was sold in handsome stoneware flagons and bottles. Securing their return for re-use was a constant challenge.

Stephen Parker's "torpedo" mineral water bottle.

Mineral water usually came in glass bottles, often in the ingenious "Codd" bottles – hence, allegedly, "codswallop" - invented in 1870 by Hiram Codd of Camberwell.

These were sealed from inside by a glass ball in the bottle neck. The ball was forced against a rubber washer by gas pressure, and could be pushed in by hand to release the contents. Many such bottles have survived, and make a satisfying rattle.

In Edwardian times national brands like Vimto, Tizer and Iron Brew (not yet Irn Bru) began to capture more and more of the market, and Coca Cola appeared in England in 1900. Bring back Zolakone, I say.

A "Codd" bottle from the Royal Marines depot.

Ginger beer bottle pictures courtesy of Ken Elks. Stephen Parker's mineral water bottle can be seen in the Deal Maritime and Local History Museum.

"Zolakone and good old ginger beer", published on 17 January 2018.

12.

Stylish advertising c.1903

As Christmas approaches businesses redouble their efforts to find new ways to draw us in. Edwardian traders in Deal had a few unusual tricks up their sleeves too.

How about, for instance, a handsome stationery cabinet for the home or business? Plain on the outside, but when you open the doors you see advertisements for eleven local businesses and schools in attractive gold lettering.

This splendid cabinet was made in the early 1900s.

A small cabinet like this, roughly 15 inches square, was designed to store notepaper, envelopes, invoices, compliment slips and the like. There was usually a drawer at the bottom for stamps and other bits and pieces.

Cabinets displaying advertisements seem to have been quite rare. It is certainly exciting to have such an unusual snapshot of some of Deal's leading traders c.1903.

Seven of these were High Street businesses. They included familiar names like the wine and spirit merchants Nethersole & Sons, the home furnisher Herbert Clarabut and the drapers and outfitters John Pittock & Son.

In October 1903 the special display at Pittocks was of Royal Worcester American Corsets costing from 3/11d to 25/- ("Perfect Models"… "Dash, Effect"… "De Luxe of the World").

Pittocks were said to be the oldest gents outfitters in the country.

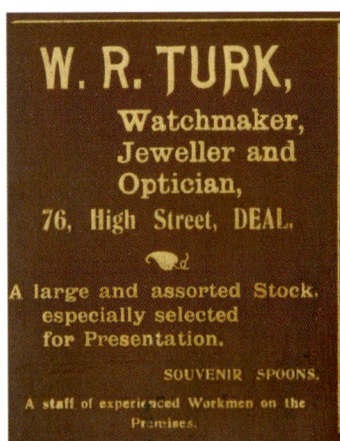

A little further north were the premises of William Turk, watchmaker, jeweller and optician, whose name is preserved – just – on the large clock still attached to 76 High Street.

Nearby, at number 86, was the chemist George Head, whose own special preparations included a Nursery Hair Lotion and a Magical Corn Cure.

Another speciality of his was an Extract of Glycerine and Cucumber which, he claimed, "effectually removes the roughness, redness, or tan caused by wind and sun, and renders the skin beautifully soft and white".

This product might well have found favour among those patronising Charles Lindsell's bicycle shop – "Cycling Taught by an Expert" – whose splendid advertisement has a prominent position in the middle of the cabinet.

South Eastern Motor and Cycle Works, BROAD STREET, DEAL.
Cycles for Sale or Hire.   Cycling Taught by an Expert.
Enamelling, Plating, and all Repairs Executed on the Premises.   C. LINDSELL, Proprietor.

Lindsell's shop stood on the corner of Middle Street and Broad Street, and as Gregory Holyoake has described (Mercury Memories 25 October), was one of the many bicycle shops in Deal and Walmer.

But Lindsell could clearly see the way the wind was blowing. Although the sign in the photograph refers to the South Eastern Cycle Works, the advertisement on the cabinet expands the name of the business to incorporate the word "Motor".

Two schools also thought it worth advertising: Deal College in Alfred Square, not long before it closed, and Miss McCormick's Bute House School for Girls ("Physical Culture a Speciality") in Victoria Road.

Charles Lindsell's South Eastern Cycle Works c1910.

But whose idea was it to commission the cabinet in the first place? Who persuaded their fellow traders to contribute to the cost of a batch of purpose made cabinets, and negotiated with the supplier?

My money is on T Steed Bayly, Mayor of Deal in 1905 and all-round mover and shaker. Not only does he advertise his High Street ironmongery on the right hand panel, and his china shop on the left, but he takes the prime position on the front of the drawer, visible even when the cabinet is closed.

Three advertisements are for businesses from outside Deal. One, with a splendid picture of a removal cart, was commissioned by Flashman & Co of Dover, estate agents, auctioneers and furniture removers "by appointment to Her Late Majesty, the Queen".

Rather more surprising is the promotion of Southport – "The Montpellier of the North" no less - and in particular of "Kenworthy's Hydropathic High-class Boarding Establishment". This had opened in 1876 and the building, complete with a sprung-floored ball-room and Southport's oldest lift, still survives.

The glittering shop front of watchmaker and jeweller William Turk.

Most curious of all is the advertisement for the Cosmopolitan Printing, Publishing & Advertising Company of Bristol. Why would the company secretary, one Walter Sing, think it worthwhile advertising in Deal?

Perhaps there is a straightforward answer – that Mr Sing's company made the cabinet. But quite how Steed Bayly of Deal, if it was he, came to do business with Walter Sing in Bristol must remain a mystery.

We shall probably never know how many Deal cabinets were made – does anyone know of any others? But it is pleasing that at least one has survived, long after all the businesses it promoted so attractively have closed their doors.

"Questions and answers behind cabinet", published on 13 December 2017.

13.

Seafront entertainment at the Pavilion

The sad saga of the Regent, sold by Dover District Council in 2011 to developers wanting to reopen it as a cinema, shows no sign of ending.

It is cold comfort to recall that Deal Council took over twenty years to agree and construct the building which would later, much modified, become the Regent.

On the other hand its transformation into a cinema in 1933 took place wonderfully quickly. If only the same could be said of its intended rebirth as a cinema 80 years later.

The Regent stands on land that once formed part of the Naval Yard. In 1876, on the initiative of the landlord of the Walmer Castle Hotel, a large roller skating rink was opened on part of the site, to the north of the Timeball Tower.

In 1892 the Council bought a piece of land to the east and built a bandstand, and in 1899 the Rink owners, the brewers Hills and Sons, built a new Walmer Castle Hotel – the one we see today – to the west. The following year a London entrepreneur in the variety business turned the Rink into an entertainment venue called the Alcazar, but it was not a success.

The Rink, with the Timeball Tower on the right.

The bandstand next to the Rink (Picture Sue Solley).

In 1901 Thompson's, the Walmer brewers, bought and closed down Hills brewery. They immediately sought ways to rid themselves of both the Walmer Castle Hotel and the Rink.

This was excellent news for councillors convinced that the development of Deal as a seaside resort depended on constructing a covered band shelter, or "Pavilion". What better location than the site of the old Rink?

The Pavillion in 1931.

Things got off to a good start. In 1904 Thompson's placed the Rink – sometimes called Marine Terrace Gardens – at the Council's disposal for a peppercorn rent. Two years later came the offer to sell. But there was a catch. The brewers would only sell the Rink if the Council also bought the Walmer Castle Hotel, its stables and an adjoining fish shop. After heated debates the Council agreed.

There was uproar. The decision became the burning issue in the 1906 local elections, with strong opposition to such "reckless expenditure"– particularly from the "Anti-Rinkite" ratepayers in North Ward.

The Council's efforts failed. The plan depended on securing a loan of £6,500. This needed Government approval. A public enquiry was held and permission was refused.

After the wet summer of 1912 badly affected attendance at band concerts plans for a covered shelter of some kind were again drawn up. This time the intention – agreed by 11 votes to 10 – was to build a pavilion on piles on the beach. It would have a 20 foot wide promenade on all sides and a bandstand on the centre of the seaward side.

Again there was huge opposition, not least from the Deal boatmen. But the Council – at considerable expense – cleared almost every hurdle. Except the last. In July 1914, only days before the outbreak of war, a Committee of the House of Lords threw out the Deal Pier and Marine Order. And that was that.

But the issue would not go away. Post-war, many still believed that the future of Deal depended on building a large covered venue for entertainments of all kinds. Alas in 1922 Thompson's yet again refused to sell the Rink independently of the Walmer Castle Hotel. Perhaps, some thought, it was time to consider building a large covered structure at the shore end of the Pier. But passions ran high and nothing could be agreed.

At last a breakthrough. Thompson's finally softened their hearts, for some reason, and agreed to gift the necessary land. In 1927 councillors resolved to build the Pavilion, though only by 12 votes to 8.

Down came the Edwardian bandstand, up went a large glass and iron structure, and in August 1928 the Pavilion was officially opened.

The management were soon organising musical and dramatic entertainments of all kinds, not to mention an evening of All-In Wrestling featuring Atholl Oakley, heavyweight champion of Great Britain, and Norman the Butcher ("the Knock-Out King").

But tastes were changing: the Council had missed the boat. By 1933 the Pavilion was losing £1,000 a year, and when two businessmen offered to rent the building and turn it into a cinema councillors jumped at the chance.

Local ratepayers, so opposed to the building of the Pavilion, now worried about its closure. Boarding house proprietors feared the impact on the summer season. Others were frankly baffled as to "the needs of modern seekers after pleasure and health".

This time the Council moved with almost indecent haste. Terms were agreed in April 1933 and Deal's new "super cinema" opened only three months later.

The Regent Cinema in the 1930s (Picture Colin Varrall).

The "Regent Cinema Theatre" could seat almost 1,000 people. A handsome portico with a white façade now extended over the old pavement forecourt. Internal decoration was in green and old-gold, with seating in four different colours.

The Regent closed as a cinema in 1963, and as a Bingo Hall in 2009. It now stands forlorn and boarded up. The Walmer Castle Hotel, on the other hand, which the brewers were so determined to palm off on the Council, is still going strong.

"Skating, wrestling and music at the Pavilion", published on 5 December 2018.

14.

The Independent Order of Oddfellows

The Royal Leisure Centre and the Royal Snooker Club in King Street occupy one of the largest buildings in central Deal. This was was previously a theatre and then a cinema.

But the clue to the origins of the building lies in the name of the path that runs alongside it: Odd Fellows Alley.

In the nineteenth century, before the modern welfare state, friendly societies became very popular and successful. They offered financial services to individuals but also mutual support and friendship. One of the largest national societies was the Independent Order of Oddfellows (Manchester Unity).

A lodge was formed in Deal in 1862 and took the name Lord Palmerston in honour of the Prime Minister of the day. Its first home was in the Rose Hotel in Lower Street (later the High Street); landlord David Almond became treasurer.

The lodge went from strength to strength. Membership rose from 161 in 1872 to 431 in 1889, with an average age of only 30. Annual highlights included lavish anniversary dinners and huge summer fetes in the grounds of Walmer Castle.

The Oddfellows' first lodge room was in the Rose Hotel.

The lodge was certainly ambitious. In 1890 the Mayor laid the foundation stone for a new Oddfellows Hall in King Street. The Mercury was delighted, and applauded the lodge for buying and demolishing the unsightly "antiquated properties" that used to stand there.

The hall opened in 1893 as a "place of public entertainment". The Oddfellows' lodge room, and initially it seems a row of shops, occupied the ground floor. Above was a large hall complete with stage, gallery, organ room and dressing rooms.

In Edwardian times live entertainments and public meetings began to give way to the showing of silent films, and the hall became known as the Theatre Royal. In 1934, fully refurbished, it reopened as the Royal Cinema. This survived until 1981.

In 1893 the Oddfellows built a large new hall in King Street.

The Oddfellows lodge continued to thrive before the First World War but the Liberal Government's 1911 National Insurance Act raised difficult questions about the role of friendly societies in the longer term.

The Oddfellows' last permanent home.

The lodge seems to have moved out of the King Street hall during the First World War. Between the wars it met in a number of different places, including the St Andrew's parish room in Duke Street.

For a time after the Second World War the lodge once again had a home of its own, meeting at the Odd Fellows (not, for some reason, Oddfellows) Hall in Century Walk. This had previously been used by the Rechabites, a temperance friendly society. It is not clear when the lodge was wound up, but by the 1990s the building was home to a nursery.

The Oddfellows however are very much still with us. "A friendship group open to everyone", there are branches in Dover and Sandwich. Enquires are warmly welcomed – please ring 0161 832 9361.

"Odd but friendly pioneers of the welfare state", published on 22 November 2017.

15.

Rounders, quoits and trap-bat at Castle Inn

A summer Saturday afternoon in Victorian Deal. What could be nicer than a stroll along the seafront towards Sandown Castle? Pause en route to admire the imposing Sandown Terrace, and the venerable Sandown windmill.

Inspecting storm damage outside the Castle Inn.

And then, near the ruins of the old castle, the welcome sight of the Castle Inn and the prospect of a glass or two of fine ale or porter brewed at Mr Hills' Deal Brewery. Or, outside, the chance to impress with one's prowess at rounders, quoits or trap-bat.

The inn was said to have served in earlier days as the canteen for the soldiers at Sandown Castle. Until 1863 it had the rather charming name of the Good Intent.

Sadly Thomas Cattermole, landlord between 1868 and 1873, was anything but charming. In 1869 he was up before the magistrates on a charge of assault ("he was not aware that he had struck the [female] complainant, as he was so full of drink...").

Cattermole had a very short fuse. The following year a street brawl led to a charge of assaulting a military policeman and the sentence of two months' hard labour. In November he was in the dock again for "shaking his fist and otherwise annoying" the chief officer of the coastguard.

Cattermole also rented out bathing machines, and in 1871 could be found complaining to the magistrates about the habit of students from Deal College bathing naked near the pub "within a few yards of my machines".

Standing half a mile north of the town, the Castle Inn was not easy for the police to supervise. Charging landlord Thomas Sladden in 1877 with serving beer out of hours, Superintendent Capps told the magistrates that he believed Sladden kept watch through a telescope for the approach of the police.

The pub was also particularly vulnerable to burglaries. In 1885, for example, two labourers were charged with stealing "about 27 pint bottles, containing ale, nine drinking glasses, a jug and six pewter measures".

Yet the greatest threat came from the sea. The pub suffered frequent storm damage at high tide, and in 1869 was completely surrounded by seawater for a time. The Deal Telegram cheerfully advised that the Castle Inn "appears sooner or later doomed to destruction".

Yet it survived, and continued to do good business. It was not until 1904 that the new owners, Thompson & Son of Walmer, decided to build a new pub set further back from the sea.

The Castle Inn remained open while the new Sandown Castle was being built. But when landlord George Tandy called it a day on the grounds that the old building had become unsafe, its fate was sealed.

The newly built Sandown Castle to the left of the old Castle Inn.

For most of the twentieth century, as Deal expanded steadily northwards, the Sandown Castle Hotel did good business with both locals and visitors.

The end came in 1986 when the brewers – now Charrington's – closed the house and put it up for sale. The building was damaged by a "mystery blaze" the following year, and subsequently demolished.

"Landlord was 'anything but charming'!", published on 22 February 2018.

16.

A remarkable discovery at the Lord Clyde

It is not unusual to come across forgotten or unexpected items when tidying a spare room or shed. Happily it is much less common when doing so to discover a human skull.

But this is what happened in 1963 to John Mantle, the newly arrived landlord of the Lord Clyde public house in Walmer, when clearing out a lumber room.

Mr Mantle also found a fragile note explaining that the skull was that of a man called Alum Bheg of the 46th Regiment of the Bengal Native Infantry. He had been "blown away from a gun" for his part in the Indian Uprising of 1857-58 (or "Mutiny" as the British termed it).

At least two newspapers – though not, as far as I can establish, the Mercury – carried the story of the find, together with a picture of Mr and Mrs Mantle holding the skull. The discovery was described as "grisly" and "nerve shattering".

For more than fifty years nothing more was heard. Then, in 2014, Dr Kim Wagner of Queen Mary University of London was contacted out of the blue by the current owners of the skull. Three years later he published an excellent book entitled "The Skull of Alum Bheg"*.

Dr Wagner tells a fascinating but grim story. In 1857 Alum Bheg had been a havildar – sergeant – with the 46th Bengal Native Infantry based in Sialkot in northern India (today, Pakistan). His regiment mutinied in July 1857 and in the turmoil several British civilians were murdered.

Mr and Mrs Mantle proudly display their find.

There is no evidence that Alum Bheg was involved in these killings, but in the aftermath of the uprising the British were in no mood to be merciful. Alum Bheg was one of six men blown apart by cannon in Sialkot on 10 July 1858. His head was then picked up as a trophy by Captain Costello of the 7th Dragoon Guards.

Later that year Costello resigned his commission and brought the skull home with him to Ireland – the explanatory note was written on notepaper from a Dublin hotel – but he seems not to have kept it for long.

How on earth did the skull come to be in the Lord Clyde?

One possibility is that Captain Costello gave or sold the skull to a fellow officer. The depot of the 7th Dragoons was in Canterbury for several years from the late 1850s, and there is even record of a troop being based at the Walmer barracks for a time in July 1871.

So perhaps the skull, having arrived in Kent with a Dragoon officer, was then acquired by the owner or tenant of the Lord Clyde. This small beerhouse, as it was then, was named after Field Marshall Sir Colin Campbell, a British hero of the uprising, probably on his death in 1863.

Lord Clyde, Field Marshall Sir Colin Campbell, after whom the pub was named.

Someone was certainly very interested in the tumultuous events that had taken place in India not long before. Perhaps acquiring the skull was another – much more macabre – manifestation of their enthusiasm.

But a better lead, as Dr Wagner observes, may be the surname "Monckton". During the uprising in Sialkot the Deputy Commissioner was one Henry Monckton. For a long period in the twentieth century the landlord of the Lord Clyde was Billy Monckton, a former Royal Marine.

When Billy took over the beerhouse in 1924 it was owned by Jude, Hanbury & Co, the Canterbury brewers. It was not until 1950 that the house, by then owned by

The Lord Clyde in 1923.

Whitbread, was awarded a full licence. Billy remained the landlord until 1960.

If a clear family link could be established between Henry and Billy Monckton the mystery of the skull's whereabouts between 1858 and 1963 and its sojourn at the Lord Clyde would come close to being solved.

If Billy had found the skull on taking over the Lord Clyde, as the Mantles did nearly 40 years later, word would surely have quickly got around. It seems much more likely that he brought with him, or later inherited, this alarming family heirloom, and into the lumber room it went in due course.

The pub in the 1950s, now owned by Whitbread.

Billy died in 1963, aged 79. John Mantle, a retired Thames tugboat captain, left the Lord Clyde the following year. Perhaps, having worked as a tug master in Bahrain for the previous ten years, life in the Lord Clyde was a little too uneventful – despite the skull.

Alum Bheg's story is told in Kim Wagner's recent book.

The Lord Clyde closed as a public house in 2010 and is now a fish and seafood restaurant (Whits of Walmer).

Dr Wagner hopes that Alum Bheg's skull will one day return to India for burial. This seems right and proper.

* *Kim A. Wagner, The Skull of Alum Bheg: The Life and Death of a Rebel of 1857 (London 2017)*

"Skull discover reveals a story of treason", published on 13 June 2018.

17.

The Rose Hotel, High Street
(with Steve Glover)

As the Mercury reported on 14 June, the Rose Hotel public house is no more. So we say goodbye to "Deal High Street's last old fashioned boozer", and hello to the Rose Hotel, bar and restaurant which opened this week.

The old Rose Hotel played an important part in the social life of Deal for over 200 years. This was particularly true in Victorian and Edwardian times, when it was a popular venue for dinners and celebrations. So in some ways the latest change of function turns the wheel full circle.

The brewery in Lower Street (now the High Street) with the Rose on the right.

The building probably dates from around 1800. In the nineteenth century it adjoined the brewery premises owned first by the Igguldens and then by the Hills family. Behind the pub lay the brewery itself, and for a long time the building next door served as the brewery offices for Hills and Sons.

The Rose – as it was originally called – was owned by the brewery. In 1901 it changed hands when Thompson & Son of Walmer bought the entire Hills estate and demolished the brewery. Fifty years later came another change when

Thompson's were taken over by Charrington's. In recent times the Rose Hotel has been a free house.

In its heyday the Rose was one of Hills' flagship pubs. The premises were extended south to include a large meeting room on the first floor, and in 1885 the brewers invested heavily in adding an extra storey to the main building.

Further improvements were made in 1891, when it was described as a Commercial Hotel, and in February 1900 came the grand opening of a new billiard saloon ("wine and spirits at bar prices").

The Rose Hotel in 1904, now with an extra storey.

All this meant that by 1900 the Rose could boast seven bedrooms, a coffee room, commercial room and billiard room on the first floor and, on the ground floor, a bar, smoking room, bar parlour and large kitchen.

There was an excellent cellar in the basement, and to the rear a coal and wood store, a "knife house" – could they have meant to say "ice house"? – a four-stall stable with a loft and a "standing stable" for five more horses.

It is not surprising that the Rose was by then one of the town's most popular venues for "smokers" – evening entertainments – and posh dinners. Some were for groups of employees like the railwaymen or George Cottew's building workers, others for clubs and societies.

Exhibition matches were held in the billiard room, and there were occasional table tennis tournaments.

Landlords worked hard to attract visitors from out of town. An advertisement from 1897 describes the Rose as "a Family and Commercial Hotel and Posting House" with a "spacious hall for public and trades' dinners [and] every comfort for golfers, cyclists, anglers etc".

Long term residents included the Lord Palmerston lodge of the Oddfellows Friendly Society. This was founded at the pub in 1862 and was based there for some thirty years. The supply of refreshment must have been a very welcome source of income.

A second local claim to fame was that the Deal and Walmer Licensed Victuallers Association was founded there in 1893. Successive landlords were active in its affairs.

This all helped to cement the reputation of the Rose as a very respectable establishment. Landlords like David Almond, who ran the pub between 1862 and 1885, or Richard Currie who went on to serve on the town council, were men of some consequence in the affairs of the town.

In earlier days the entertainment provided was less conventional. This included the display of the tattooed head of a New Zealand chief, with visitors paying 6d a time. (Advertising for a subsequent exhibition in Ramsgate may have had little impact, the trophy having been described as a Sheep's Head rather a Chief's Head.)

In 1863 fire threatened the pub when clothes placed on a chair were set alight by a candle. The occupants of the room, having escaped suffocation, then had the indignity of being described by the Deal Telegram as "Miss Meacham, the fat young giantess, and her sister".

The Rose and its customers do not seem to have given the magistrates much cause for concern over the years. In 1858 two rival sweeps were involved in a fight in the tap room, but there are few other examples of trouble.

The pub in 1952.

Landlords did sometimes find themselves up before the Bench. In 1882 David Almond was fined for "selling whisky below the standard". In 1893 Percy Edwards had the same misfortune – or tried the same stunt – when his whisky and gin were found to be "not of the substance and quality demanded".

In 1915 landlord Samuel Dodsworth had the distinction of being charged under the Defence of the Realm Act when a large number of soldiers were found drinking beer outside the permitted hours.

In the twentieth century the Rose began to lose its position as a favoured venue for functions and dinners, and at some point

The pub interior in its final days.

the hall in the annex next door stopped being used. The billiard table disappeared and in due course a pool table, dart board and eventually cable television appeared downstairs.

The house continued to offer bed and breakfast accommodation for many years but had by now evolved into a friendly no-frills public house – of the kind now fast disappearing across the country, alas.

In the words of Steve Plews, the last landlord, the Rose Hotel "survived on wet sales alone which was something to be proud of. It [was] a proper drinker's pub".

The pub still made the news once in a while. In 1969 the Mercury reported that Tubbs, a cat belonging to landlady Margo Thompson, managed to get stuck in the rafters of St George's church next door and needed to be rescued by the RSPCA.

A connection with St George's of a different kind came in 1989 with the imaginative commissioning by Charrington's of a new pub sign painted by their artist (and Deal resident) Bill Pierce.

It shows two of the roses associated with Reverend Henry D'Ombrain, vicar of St George's, who founded the Rose Society and was its secretary for twenty five years. Hopefully the sign will also be restored and preserved.

"Pub 'goes full circle' ahead of re-opening", published on 25 April 2018.

The sign board showed a red Bourbon rose.

18.

The Swan Hotel, Queen Street
(with Steve Glover)

The old Hole in the Roof, which re-opens this weekend as the Queen Street Tap, can claim to be Deal's oldest pub – if one ignores the fact that the premises were completely rebuilt in the 1930s.

In 1890 workmen repairing the building found a stone dated 1694. It is likely that the Five Bells, as it then was, did indeed date back to the seventeenth century. Certainly its position in the magistrates' registers suggests that by 1820 only the Black Horse on Lower Street was thought to be older.

The Swan Hotel, c. 1910, with a pony and trap.

In the eighteenth century the Five Bells not only served beer but brewed it as well. This was very common in Georgian times. In some parts of the country "brew pubs" flourished for another hundred years, but in nineteenth century Kent the breweries came to dominate the drink trade.

The Five Bells stood on what was then Five Bells Lane. This became Queen Street around 1800, and in the 1820s landlord Brockman Beal changed the name of the pub to the Swan. By now the house was owned by the larger of the two Deal breweries.

Beal promoted his house as a "Commercial Inn and Posting House", and certainly the success of the Swan Hotel – as it soon formally became – was based on the accommodation, stables and carriage space it could offer to visitors, and on the hiring of ponies and traps.

In 1838 the Swan's outbuildings could accommodate 20 horses and six coaches, and many more animals could be packed into the yard if necessary. In 1900 the hotel itself had eight bedrooms, and on the ground floor a "commercial room", sitting room, smoking room, a bar with two entrances and a bar parlour.

Nationally the arrival of the railways usually marked the decline of the large coaching inns. But the opening of the line from Deal to Minster in 1847, and the decision to build the station round the corner from the Swan, seem if anything to have boosted its fortunes.

It did its reputation no harm that Charles Dickens was said to have stayed there when visiting the town to witness the opening of the new line.

In 1887 landlord Arthur Webster took pains to set out his stall (so to speak) in the local directory: "very old established, one minute from the station, family & commercial, livery & bait stables, ponies & traps, masonic banquets & garden parties etc supplied with every necessary".

Some landlords had other strings to their bows. George Rolfe was a horse dealer – which made sense – while his successor in 1871, Vernon Brown from Australia, also traded as a wine and spirits merchant and "agent for Webb's Superior Mineral Water of Islington".

Patrons of the Swan pose before a charabanc outing – men only.

Soft drinks almost proved the Swan's downfall. In 1881 fire broke out at an adjacent building used to bottle mineral water and spread to one of the hotel stables.
The flames were eventually quenched but a horse worth 200 guineas belonging to Sanger's circus had to be put down.

The house seems generally to have been well run, but trouble could still occur. In 1842, for example, the Watch Committee awarded PC Edward Browning £1.10s.0d in compensation for injuries sustained in the line of duty when confronting a belligerent soldier in the Swan.

In 1908 Eliza Mackenzie was given a week's hard labour for drunkenness at the Swan "in company with a gentleman from the fleet". In response to her claim that she had intended to lead him back to his ship the magistrate commented dryly that "I have no doubt you were going to lead him on".

In 1874 the brewers, Hills and Sons, refurbished parts of the hotel and added a smoking room. The work was carried out by the local builders W & G Denne at the modest cost of £59.10s.

In 1901 Thompson & Son of Walmer bought the Hills brewery estate, took possession of the Swan and advertised their ownership and their products on a large sign on the side wall. The change of ownership and beer aside, business probably continued much as before.

The rebuilt Swan looking east down Queen Street.

The Swan is a rare example of a Deal pub to have been completely rebuilt between the two world wars. The initiative came from the Council, who persuaded the reluctant brewers to demolish the old building to facilitate the widening of Queen Street.

In April 1937 the Mercury carried a rather poignant notification of the auction of superfluous items from the old building. These included "mirrors and overmantles, antique Trafalgar seat, easy Windsor and other chairs, excellent Pianoforte, pictures, copper spirit jugs… and a nearly new 5-pull Beer Engine".

The Swan in 1952, now owned by Charrington's.

The new Swan Hotel soon took the place of the old, set back several feet from the original site. Thompson's could at least now boast of "a thoroughly up-to-date hotel in every respect… hot and cold water in every bedroom… handsomely and comfortably furnished throughout".

Thompson's were swallowed up by Charrington's in the early 1950s but the Swan Hotel it remained until the name was shortened to Swans in 1985.

In May 1997 Swans in turn became the Hole in the Roof, and a £160,000 refit followed in 1999. Over the years it became a popular and successful live music venue.

The Hole in the Roof c. 2009.

The original name of the previous building, Five Bells, was later taken up by a pub in Middle Street. This closed in 1959. It nearly made a welcome return as the name of Wetherspoon's new pub in Queen Street, but a local campaign persuaded the company to call it the Sir Norman Wisdom instead.

Steve Glover is the author, with Michael Rogers, of The Old Pubs of Deal and Walmer (with Kingsdown and Mongeham).

Andrew Sargent is the author of Drinking in Deal: Beer, Pubs and Temperance in an East Kent Town, 1830 – 1914.

"Many changes through pub's long history", published on 23 August 2017.

19.

A staggeringly corrupt by-election

Allegations of electoral foul play make the headlines every now and then. But we can be sure that any wrongdoing during the current general election will be as nothing compared to the bare-faced corruption practised in Victorian Deal and Sandwich.

Between 1832 and 1885 the parliamentary borough of Sandwich, which included Deal and Walmer, was a two-member constituency. Elections were rumbustious affairs, with inducements to electors ranging from extensive "treating" – free food and drink – to downright bribery. It was therefore bitterly disappointing when the 1880 general election saw the two sitting Liberal MPs elected without a contest. But then came the joyous news that the senior MP had accepted a peerage and a by-election would be needed.

The fun started straight away when the Conservative agent arrived from London with a heavy bag of gold and quickly hired no fewer than 71 committee rooms in Deal and Walmer pubs. Almost all of them were completely superfluous, but such generosity was an excellent way of making friends and influencing people.

The Liberal's central committee room was in the Star and Garter.

The Liberals soon followed suit, but were playing catch-up. The going rate for a room in a pub was £5. This was the equivalent of four months rent or more.

The landlord of the Rose and Crown on Beach Street even contrived to rent the inside of his pub to the Liberals and the outside, for posters, to the Conservatives.

No wonder that when it was all over he expressed the fervent wish to see another election the following week.

Soon Deal and Sandwich were festooned with banners and bunting: blue for the Liberals and red for the Conservatives. Posters plastered the fronts of pubs, and as many other blank walls as the well paid poster-stickers could get away with.

The Conservative candidate, Crompton Roberts, set up his central committee room in the Royal Hotel, while Sir Julian Goldsmid for the Liberals chose the Star and Garter just up the road.

One way of getting money into the pockets of electors was to pay massively over the odds for services rendered: making a banner, say, or erecting a flag pole, or guarding a flag pole, or even (it was said) for pulling one down so that someone could be amply rewarded for putting it up again.

And then there was downright, unapologetic bribery: £3 straight away with £2 promised after the election and no questions asked. Publicans were at the heart of the many local networks of corruption that spread across the constituency, handing out gold sovereigns to favoured customers and friends.

Henry Spears of the Antwerp (now the Bohemian) for example received £108 to bribe in the Conservative interest plus £6 for canvassing and £5 for a committee room.

Sir Julian Goldsmid, the Liberal candidate.

Stephen Pritchard at the Eagle kept some of the Liberal gold intended for bribes for himself. He earned, in a later cross-examination, the memorable rebuke that "bribery is bad enough, but theft is worse".

The landlord of the Rose and Crown was happy to take money from both sides.

But for a while it was Christmas, New Year and Easter come all at once. Shopkeepers, publicans, boatmen – anyone who had a vote or might influence someone who did – had a wonderful time. And there is no sign that any of their "betters" – the clergy, councillors and magistrates of the town – raised any objections.

It was too good to last. The Conservative candidate won the election but the Liberal candidate appealed the result (and was almost universally condemned for doing so).

Crompton Roberts' victory was overturned and a Parliamentary Commission was set up to look at the extent of corruption in the parliamentary borough. Witness after witness appeared to explain in detail their part in the shenanigans, fortified by the likelihood of immunity from prosecution if they told the full truth.

The figures in the Commission's report are breathtaking. 128 people were found to have offered bribes and 1,005 – half the electorate – to have accepted them. 27 cheerfully accepted bribes from both sides.

The Commissioners themselves could scarcely believe it. They concluded that there had been "a general expectation that money would be distributed in bribery [and an] almost universal willingness and even avidity to accept bribes".

Indeed the main reason there was little illegal "treating" was that direct bribery was found to be so much more acceptable and straightforward.

The landlord of the Antwerp (right) received three months in prison for bribing electors.

But surely the recent introduction of the secret ballot must have made a difference? Not at all: "on the contrary, while it enabled many voters to take bribes on both sides it did not... render a single person unwilling to bribe for fear of bribing in vain".

Eight men from Deal and Walmer were subsequently tried and sent to prison. These included three landlords, a solicitor and the coach and fly proprietor Samuel Olds.

Fellow citizens were outraged not at their villainy but at their punishment. When John Mackins, landlord of the Stag and coxswain of the Walmer lifeboat, returned home "flags flew from the masts of all the boats in Walmer and cannon gave him a thundering salute".

Electors as a whole lost the right to be represented in Parliament, and ratepayers had to stump up over £2,000 to meet the Commission's costs. Not long afterwards the hiring of committee rooms in pubs during elections was made illegal across the country.

The citizens of Deal, Sandwich and Walmer were luckier than they probably deserved. In 1885 they found themselves able to vote once more, though now as part of the new and much larger single-member constituency of St Augustine's.

But the good times were over. Many more men now had the vote. Even the most corrupt or wealthy politician contesting the constituency would have to think twice about bribery when faced with over 12,000 voters.

Politicians continued to make inducements to electors. But these had now to take the form of promises and commitments rather than golden guineas or gallons of free beer.

A full account of the 1880 election scandal can be found in: Andrew Sargent's Drinking in Deal: Beer, Pubs and Temperance in an East Kent Town 1830 – 1914 (BooksEast, 2016).

William Licence, landlord of the Saracen's Head, bribed seventeen people for the Conservatives.

Coxswain and landlord John Mackins (right) was also sent to prison for bribery.

"An election full of corruption, bribery and cheating", published on 7 June 2017

20.

The Cinque Ports Artillery Volunteers

Sharp-eyed visitors to Sandwich Quay may spot a stone on the front wall of the drill hall, until recently used by the Army Cadets, which reads "2nd CPAV AD1869". They would probably pass by none the wiser.

The Sandwich drill shed was opened in 1869.

Should they later happen to stroll down Hope Road in Deal they would find enlightenment. Above the entrance to the drill hall now used by the 2235 (Deal) Squadron of the Air Training Corps a less cryptic plaque reads: "Cinque Ports Artillery Volunteers 1878". No doubt these were fine bodies of men, but who were they?

In 1859 Lord Derby's Government, alarmed at rising tensions in Europe and by the state of Britain's defences, authorised the creation of local volunteer rifle and artillery "corps". By 1860 more than 120,000 men had enrolled.

Enthusiasm often outran efficiency. In 1861 a march to Sandwich by the newly formed Deal and Walmer Rifle Corps became shambolic as men fell out to take unauthorised refreshment at the Coach and Horses. Several others tumbled into a stream in pursuit of a rabbit. This particular corps proved to be only a very temporary addition to the nation's defences.

More permanent were the artillery corps which sprang up around the Kent coast. A public meeting in November 1859 resolved to form a local corps for Deal and Walmer and the following February the 3rd Corps of the Cinque Ports Artillery Volunteers came into being.

The Deal and Walmer drill shed is still in use today.

Another CPAV corps was formed in Sandwich the following month. In all six corps were formed in Kent maritime towns, and in 1862 brigade headquarters were established in Dover.

Volunteers had to drill at least 24 times a year to be rated as "effective". They paid subscriptions, and many had also to contribute to the cost of uniforms and equipment. Nonetheless, across the country, probably one man in twelve served with the volunteers at some point in his lifetime.

In the early days NCOs and sometimes officers might be elected by the men themselves. In 1861, for example, the 3rd CPAV elected their two sergeants by ballot – one for Deal and one for Walmer.

Both local CPAV corps had an authorised strength of 80 NCOs and men, together with a Captain, 1st Lieutenant and 2nd Lieutenant.

Although artillerymen, volunteers were trained to shoot with rifles, and the Sandwich corps seems to have been particular proficient. Shooting competitions were very competitive, not least because of the glittering array of prizes on offer.

In 1878 the prizes awarded to deserving volunteers from Deal and Walmer included a dinner service, a silver watch, inkstands, an 18 gallon cask of beer (courtesy of Hills, the local brewers), a seal-skin cap, three pairs of braces, a shoulder of mutton and six tins of lobster.

Alfred Simmons, a Sandwich builder, won the Rye Cup Challenge in 1891 (Boyer Collection).

Bugler Pittock, a Sandwich volunteer (Boyer Collection).

And who could resist the chance of winning the Ladies Challenge Trophy, a "miniature 18lb siege cannon, mounted, beautifully wrought in silver, placed on a stand of black marble" and weighing a hefty 40lbs, so generously presented by the woman of Deal?

As now, rain could sometimes spoil things. In 1868 Deal and Walmer volunteers competing for their annual prizes were soaked to the skin. But spirits rose when the corps adjoined to the Castle Inn "where the health of the ladies who had generously subscribed to the funds was proposed and drunk with great enthusiasm".

Both local corps had their ups and downs but by the 1870s had become more efficient. A key improvement was the provision of purpose-built premises in which to train and store equipment.

The Sandwich "drill shed" was built in 1869 next to Fisher Gate, and paid for by Sir Walter James, later Lord Northbourne. It was built of yellow brick, with grey brick dressings; English Heritage sees a "subtle Gothic Revival touch" in the front elevation. The hall later included a 75 foot long firing range.

The Deal shed, constructed by the local builder George Cottew, was opened with little fanfare in 1878. Drills had previously taken place in several different venues, most recently in the garden of the Deal Castle public house.

Landlord William Pettet was probably the only landlord in Deal to have had a working artillery piece on the premises. He may have been glad to be rid of it, but probably not to lose the custom of the thirsty volunteer gunners who looked after it.

Private Goodbon also served with the Sandwich corps (Boyer Collection).

Up the hill in Walmer the enthusiastic brewer Morris Thompson, 2nd Lieutenant of his local corps, had earlier shown his zeal for the cause by christening one of his Dover Road pubs the Cinque Ports Volunteer.

CPAV corps were issued with a variety of artillery pieces. These were rarely state of the art. In 1870 the Sandwich drill shed was home to two 50 cwt 24 pounders "on garrison standby carriages" and two 38 cwt 18 pounders on travelling carriages.

Volunteers were sometimes as a treat allowed to train on the huge 10 and 9 inch muzzle loaders in Dover. But for most of the century their basic weapon was the Armstrong rifled 40 pounder.

It was the fate of volunteer units to be repeatedly renamed. The 3rd Corps in Deal and Walmer, for example, became the 5th Corps in 1870, No. 7 Battery of the 1st CPAV in 1880 and No.6 Company in 1890. In 1902 the various CPAV corps were attached to the Royal Garrison Artillery.

A CPAV officer in full dress (Boyer Collection).

The story of the Volunteers ends in 1908 with the creation of the Territorial Force, the forerunner of the modern Territorial Army. The Sandwich detachment found itself joining units from Ramsgate and Margate to form the No. 3 Battery of the 3rd Home Counties (Cinque Ports) Brigade. Whether they were one of the volunteer units to hold a "funeral service" is not recorded.

Their Deal comrades certainly took it as a compliment to be joined with the two Dover units to form the No.1 Battery "and thus have the distinct advantage of being attached to the headquarters Battery".

There was more good news. The new brigade was allocated to the Royal Field Artillery rather than to the Royal Garrison Artillery. This meant goodbye to "slow heavy howitzer work" and the opportunity for "neat, sharp work" with field guns. So it was as field artillerymen that the Deal, Walmer and Sandwich territorials left their homes in 1914 and boarded troopships to India to relieve units of the regular army for service on the Western Front.

With thanks to Colin Varrall, Sandwich Guildhall Museum and the Kent History and Library Centre.

"Artillery gun drills held in pub garden", published on 15 November 2017.

21.

Civil Defence in 1940

Last November we remembered the Armistice which, a hundred years before, ended the battlefield carnage of the Great War. When in 1939 Britain again found itself at war the expectation was that, this time, civilians would also suffer enormous casualties.

An ARP warden, still in pyjamas and slippers, reports for duty.

After all, hadn't Prime Minister Stanley Baldwin warned in 1932 that "the bomber will always get through".

Yet for nine months, in the west at least, not much happened. Even a front line town like Deal faced the challenge of sustaining the morale and dedication of the many volunteer members of the civil defence teams.

One solution was a special home-made magazine of news and entertainment. First produced in February 1940, the chance survival of the April edition shines a light on civil defence in Deal shortly before, at last, "the balloon went up".

The leading article ("Know Your Local Civil Defence Organisation") described the work of the Auxiliary Fire Service (AFS). This included over 220 part-time firemen, drivers, messengers and motor and pedal cyclists.

The main AFS station was at the Town Hall, with other stations in Mill Road and in Dover Road opposite the Hawksdown garage. Equipment supplied by the Home Office included two heavy pumps able to discharge 700-900 gallons of water a minute.

Working alongside the AFS were the Air Raid Precaution (ARP) wardens distributed between nine posts in Deal and Walmer.

Rescue Services and First Aid Parties were based at the Cemetery Road depot, Foresters Hall in North Barrack Road and the hall in Nelson Street.

According to the author of the article many stations and posts were "rapidly becoming small club centres for personnel", complete with dart boards, table tennis tables and wireless sets donated by well-wishers.

Wardens from Post 5 (Walmer Green) on a training exercise.

On 18 March the final rounds of the Pargeter Challenge Cup for Darts – a six monthly competition for civil defence personnel, both men and women – were held in Nelson Hall. In the closely contested final W Amos (Foresters Hall) beat E Twyman (Nelson Hall) 2 to 1.

Football matches and concerts also helped to sustain morale. A concert in late March at St George's Hall included sketches and "a very unusual and amusing question bee between a ladies' and a men's team". (The men won 5 to 3.)

The April magazine also included a selection of humorous stories, poems and cartoons (several of which are reproduced here).

There was also the following "true story":
Doctor to Candidate – "If you dragged a man out of some wreckage and found him to be suffering from a fractured base of skull, what would you do?"

Candidate – "I'd put him back again and look for someone with a broken collar bone. I can treat that".

But, training aside, there was very little real work to be done. It was not until March that ARP Post No. 1 (on the Marina) proudly claimed the distinction of sending the first report of an actual bombing – of ships in the Channel – to the control centre.

Warden Neeve (Post 5) is caught napping.

The ambulance depot in Nelson Hall had earlier been transformed into a "miniature base hospital" to care for survivors of the Dunbar Castle, sunk after striking a mine near the North Goodwins. But in the event not many survivors were landed nearby.

It must have been hard to stay enthusiastic and alert. The population of the town had fallen by half, defences were being strengthened and volunteers trained. But would anything actually happen?

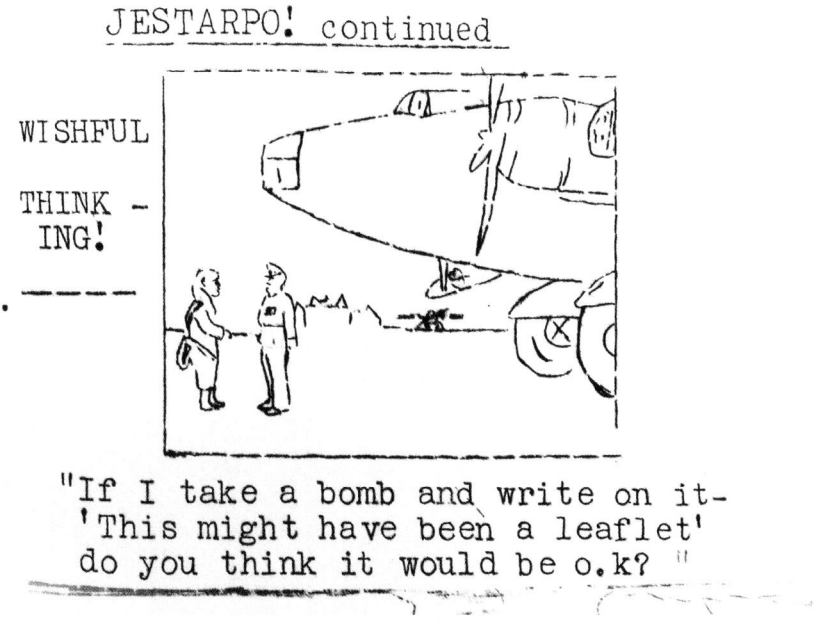

Dropping leaflets on Germany was widely ridiculed.

Why, come to that, were the RAF dropping leaflets on Germany and not bombs?

It may have seemed like a "phoney war". But at sea and in the air young men were already losing their lives.

On 2 March the Mercury reported the death of Leading Aircraftman George Peterson of Stanley Road, Deal. He had died in a crash off the Scottish coast. Experts consider his Saunders-Roe flying boat a "flawed design", and it certainly had a high accident rate.

Three weeks later 19 year old George Rose was killed in another flying accident. He had been, said his parents, Mr and Mrs Rose of Cannon Road, "very keen on his work, and was particularly proud of his badge as a gunner".

And indeed, by the time the April edition of the magazine appeared the war was becoming "phoney" no longer. On 9 April the Germans invaded Norway, and soon British soldiers were fighting and dying in a botched effort to stem the advance.

A warden in gas mask and gum boots cleans up.

A month later came the offensive in the west and within a few weeks the evacuation from Dunkirk.

Deal really was now in the front line, and civil defence a deadly serious matter. Was there any longer, I wonder, the time or inclination to produce a light-hearted monthly news magazine?

Over the next four years 65 men, women and children in Deal and Walmer lost their lives from bombs and shelling. 256 people were injured and 173 properties completely destroyed.

On 8 May 1945 Germany surrendered unconditionally, and on Sunday 1 July men and women of the borough civil defence organisations assembled in Victoria Park to parade through the town for the last time.

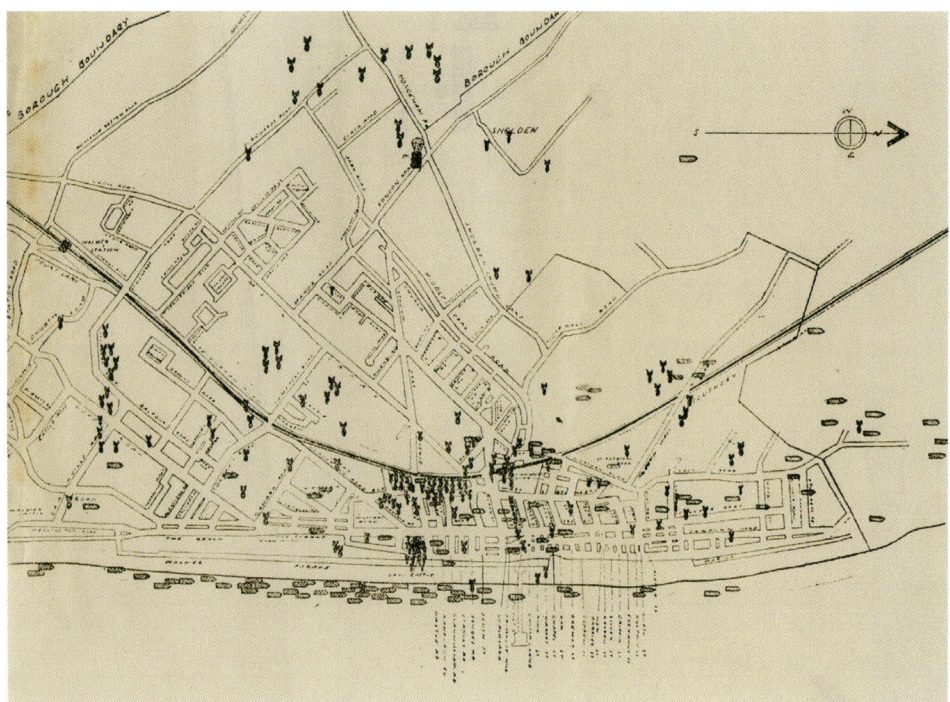

The incidence of bombs, shells and mines in central Deal.

"Local magazine shared home front news", published on 7 August 2019.

22.

Sandwich Prison 1829 – 1879

With conditions in Britain's prisons again making headlines it may be timely to remember what prison life was like in the nineteenth century for men like Thomas Bailey, an 18-year old Deal boatman sentenced in 1869 to three weeks' hard labour for causing damage at the Star public house in Middle Street.

Bailey was furious, having expected to get away with a fine. As soon as he was released he returned to the Star and took his revenge by assaulting the landlady. Back he went to prison, this time for two months' hard labour.

Sandwich prison looking from the Mill Wall. The man in the top hat is probably the prison governor, Lewis Hill.

Deal police station had a temporary lock-up. But wrong-doers given custodial sentences by the magistrates had to be sent up the coast to Sandwich. The prison there had been built in 1829 and stood near the Mill Wall a short distance from St Clement's church.

Bailey would have found himself incarcerated with twenty or more other men and women – in 1872 the average number at any one time was 21 – and would probably have shared a cell.

His fellow prisoners would have been a mixed bunch – labourers and others from the Sandwich area, but also a good many young "refractory seamen". These were merchant seaman put ashore, usually at Deal, for refusing their duty in protest at conditions on board.

In earlier times Bailey would probably have shared the prison with a large group of soldiers. In June 1841, for example, the prisoners included 17 soldiers, many of whom had offended while serving in the county with the 34th (Cumberland) Regiment of Foot.

The Sandwich "Gaol and House of Correction" was one of more than 100 local prisons in England run by individual counties or boroughs. It had 18 cells, four day rooms, two rooms for the prison staff, a large kitchen and a washroom. Outside were four "airing yards" and, at least in the early years, a prison garden.

In 1850 the prison inspectors found the prison clean, the prisoners "clean and neat" and the governor very efficient. But there was one "great deficiency", namely the failure to provide adequately for the moral and religious instruction of the prisoners.

It is hard to believe that Thomas Bailey derived much benefit from the instruction he received in 1869. But the Sabbath did at least bring some relief from the punishing regime of hard labour. In Sandwich this took the form of a treadwheel. Prisoners walked on top of a large wheel, holding a bar, and so "climbed" thousands of feet a day.

Prisoners trudging round the Brixton treadwheel in 1822.

This served no purpose other than to punish. Advocates were particularly enthusiastic about the way it could, allegedly, extract "an inescapable, exact, uniform and desired quantity of hard labour".

In 1830 prison rules required the governor to ensure that no prisoner had to climb more the 12,000 feet a day – that is, not more than the equivalent of climbing Ben Nevis, from sea level, two and a half times a day. Three years after Bailey's two incarcerations, the governor reported to the Home Office that prisoners were required to walk the treadwheel for 10 hours a day – but for only 8 hours in winter.

Unlike Dover prison, Sandwich did not offer the equally pointless alternatives of lifting iron cannon-balls ("shot drill") or turning a crank. The latter operated a mechanism which lifted a heavy weight. A warder outside the cell could adjust the weight by turning a screw. Hence, it seems, "screw" entered the lexicon of prison slang as a term for a warder.

Bailey could not have undertaken sustained hard labour on the treadwheel without a relatively generous diet. In the early days of the prison this amounted, each week, to 8 ¾ pounds of bread, 1 ½ pounds of mutton, 14 quarts of oatmeal gruel, 3 quarts of soup ("made from Meat boiled the preceding day") and 7 pounds of potatoes with pepper and salt.

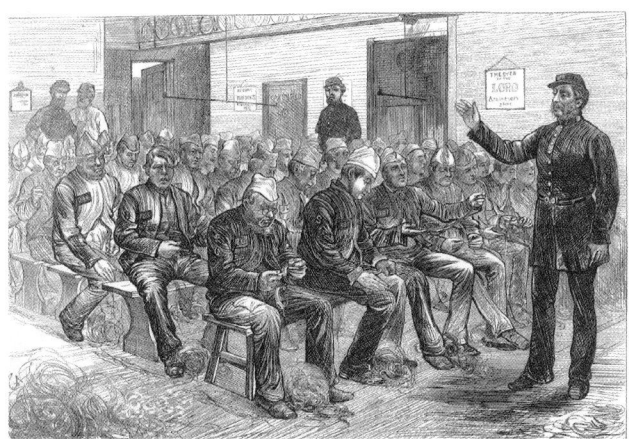
Picking oakum in a London prison.

Bailey's fellow male prisoners not sentenced to hard labour might be put to mat-making or the picking of oakum – a difficult and painful activity. The oakum, recycled from old tarry ropes and cordage, was then used to pack the joints of the timbers of wooden vessels.

Women were also incarcerated at Sandwich. One such was the pregnant 23-year old noted by the inspectors in 1850 to be awaiting trial at the Deal Quarter Sessions for stealing "a carpet and four silver spoons". Female prisoners were usually set to work washing and mending clothes – activities with which they were no doubt wearily familiar outside the prison walls.

The governor was assisted by a matron (who was often his wife) and by a "turnkey". Some prison rules seem to have been relatively humane. In 1830 new inmates were to be supplied with a full set of clothing including, for women, neckerchief, pocket handkerchief, cap and "stays when the prisoner has been in the habit of wearing them".

Prisoners were entitled "to wash thoroughly at least once every day… and to get into a tepid bath at least once each month… a sufficient supply of soap and combs being provided".

Women picking oakum.

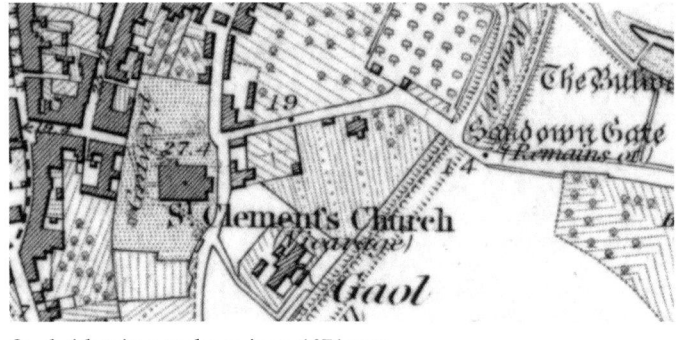

Sandwich prison as shown in an 1871 map.

In early years town councillors and the governor had a great deal of discretion in how their prison was run. But legislation in the 1860s and 1870s gradually removed local flexibility, and defined the duty of gaolers in detail.

Eight years after Thomas Bailey spent time within the prison walls, climbing the treadwheel day after day, the Government took complete control of all prisons. Sandwich prison was closed, and prisoners henceforth served their terms in Canterbury or Maidstone.

The demolition of the prison in 1879.

We do not know if Bailey's punishments had any effect in curbing his violent behaviour. If not, he would have risked being sucked into a national penal system that was in some respects even harsher than the local system he had already sampled. It was not until 1898, almost thirty years after Bailey plodded on and on, that the use of treadwheels was finally abolished.

"The hard life of a 19th century prisoner", published 12 January 2017.

23.

"Refractory seamen" withdraw their labour

Dozens of merchant ships are visible on the horizon, at anchor in the Downs.

In July 1871 seven seamen from the *Balaklava*, bound for Canada with a cargo of cement from Gravesend, were brought before the Deal magistrates. They were charged with having "wilfully and negligently" refused their duty while the ship lay at anchor in the Downs.

The vessel was only five years old and had just been corked and repaired in a London dry-dock. But John Bass, speaking for the seamen, claimed the *Balaklava* was poorly rigged, made an alarming amount of water and was altogether unseaworthy.

Having heard from the ship's master and carpenter the magistrates declared the complaint "very frivolous", and sentenced the men to a month's hard labour in Sandwich gaol. The *Balaklava* was taken on to Portsmouth for further inspection. It finally set out to cross the Atlantic in September. Three days out of Plymouth it sprang a serious leak and sank.

The case of the *Balaklava* became a cause célèbre, particularly when taken up by Samuel Plimsoll, the passionate campaigner for maritime safety. The local MP, Edward Knatchbull-Hugessen, later felt obliged to write to The Times to deny Plimsoll's claim that the magistrates had been willing in effect to send men to their deaths.

The *Balaklava*, Knatchbull-Hugessen asserted, had shipped relatively little water when in the Downs. Moreover the men had refused extra pay to take the ship on to Portsmouth for inspection, a passage safely accomplished with a scratch crew. This probably included several Deal boatmen – "runners" in the parlance of the day.

The seven men sent to Sandwich gaol were then called "refractory seamen"– that is, seamen who refused their duty under the 1854 Merchant Shipping Act. They were usually at the start of a long outbound voyage, having been paid a month's wages before leaving port. But discontent could lead to a formal complaint to the master and to a strike or go-slow on reaching the Downs. If the issue could not be resolved on board the men were taken ashore to appear before the magistrates.

Their complaint was usually that the ship was undermanned or unseaworthy – as indeed was all too often the case among the huge number of Victorian merchant vessels. For some men a spell in prison was a price worth paying for returning to dry land: "thank you", said the spokesman for 14 refractory seamen from the *Anglesea* after being given one month's hard labour in 1874, "our lives are safe there and they are not in the ship".

Or the complaints might be about living conditions. But it took a lot to soften the magistrates' hearts. When men from the *Illovo*, bound for Natal, complained of soaking bedding and uneatable food the magistrates had no sympathy: "it was well known that [there had been] very boisterous weather, and at such times as these sailors must expect a little discomfort ".

Fourteen members of the barque Edeline received 3 weeks hard labour.

It was equally clear to the magistrates that the crew of the *Edeline*, refusing to sail in what the Board of Trade surveyor said was one of the finest vessels ever built, were simply "not possessed of the pluck and courage that distinguished old British Seamen".

Then there was the sensitive seaman from the brig *Spring* who complained in 1875 that the forecastle smelt horribly of what he felt sure were the inaccessible corpses of poisoned rats. The Board of Trade surveyor ruled that the smell was caused by bilge water and added, discouragingly, that the smell "would in all probability remain there the entire voyage".

Some complaints were more bizarre. Later in 1875 Edward Blown, a Deal man, complained that a tooth had been nailed to the forecastle door of the steamship *Ardenconnel* beneath a sign reading "This is the boatswain's tooth". John Currey backed him up, but having previously refused to proceed to sea after a vision that the ship was "crooked" received five weeks hard labour.

Currey had also complained that, of all things, "there were too many Dutchmen on board". Some ships were certainly multi-cultural. Among the crew of the *Angelsea* were Norwegians, Swedes, Prussians, Russians and Finns, some of whom utterly failed to persuade the magistrates of the unreasonableness of having to work on the Sabbath.

In fact it was extremely rare for the magistrates to find in favour of striking seaman. Testimony from the ship's master was usually believed, and complaints about what would today seem intolerable or criminally dangerous working conditions were dismissed as trivial or mischievous.

The Lothair, a tea clipper later converted to a barque, was another frequent visitor to the Downs.

But as E C Pain commented dryly in 1929 "what seemed to impress the good people of Deal in those days was not the injustice done to the men imprisoned under such circumstances, so much as the hardship imposed on long-suffering ratepayers in being called upon to maintain them".

If a dispute occurred in a ship lying off Walmer the cost of any prison sentence would be charged to Cinque Ports funds, and if south of Walmer Castle the county would pick up the tab. But most ships in the Downs lay off Deal, which meant that cases were heard by the borough magistrates and the council had to foot the bill.

By the 1870s numbers had got out of hand. In February 1875 the Town Clerk, writing to the Board of Trade, reported that 111 seamen had been sent to prison in 1874 by the Deal and Cinque Ports magistrates. This was three times as many as all other offenders, and cost ratepayers between £300 and £400.

The cook of the Ambassador was sent to Dover gaol after complaining that the galley fire would not burn properly.

The Deal Telegram, happy to fan the flames, pointed out that the cost of incarcerating a seaman in Sandwich gaol – 10s 6d a week – was twice that of maintaining a law-abiding but destitute citizen in the Eastry Workhouse. It claimed, rather implausibly, that "men actually get fat on gaol treatment; they look upon it as an agreeable relaxation from their ordinary business".

On the other hand, in the rare cases when the magistrates found in favour of the refuseniks, the upshot might be a complaint by the shipowner to the Secretary of State that maintaining discipline had been sacrificed to penny-pinching.

Surely, argued the town, central government should foot the prison bill. After all, none of this was Deal's fault. And the town derived little or no benefit from the presence of these ships in the Downs. Most were engaged in long-distance trade and had been fully provisioned before leaving port.

Relief finally came in an unexpected way. In 1878 the Government took responsibility for all prisons and closed Sandwich gaol. The cost of maintaining prisoners sentenced by local magistrates, for whatever reason, would no longer fall on the town.

For seamen a major turning point was the passing of the 1876 Merchant Shipping Act. This gave the Board of Trade much stronger powers of inspection and introduced what quickly became known as the "Plimsoll line" to show safe loading limits.

A tribute to Samuel Plimsoll in The Graphic (1875).

Although initially left to individual shipowners to decide where the line should be – one is said to have painted it on the funnels of his ships – the positioning was fixed by law in the 1890s. Today's international load lines are more complicated but still make an important and visible contribution to maritime safety.

The fate of the men who sailed in the *Balaklava* back in 1871 was much less grim than it might have been. Plimsoll had claimed that the ship had sunk in September with all hands. In fact all 16 members of the replacement crew had been rescued by a Spanish ship.

The seven refractory seaman sent off to Sandwich gaol in July, who according to E C Pain were released early by order of the Board of Trade, would nonetheless have felt thoroughly vindicated.

"Our lives are safe in gaol - they are not safe in the ship", published 16 August 2017.

24.

Cheating boatmen

Events in Deal did not often attract national attention in Victorian times. Unfortunately when they did it was usually for the wrong reasons.

In 1880 it was the massively corrupt by-election, which led to the constituency being disenfranchised. Earlier, in the 1860s, it had been the discreditable behaviour of certain Deal boatmen, William Spears and William Middleton in particular.

"South-end" boats, with the pier in the background.

The 1860s were a relatively good time for the 400 or so Deal boatmen. It was a hard and dangerous occupation, but there could sometimes be large rewards.

The most celebrated bonanza came in 1866 when the *Iron Crown*, homeward bound from Shanghai with a valuable cargo, struck the Goodwin Sands. The ship was saved with the help of lifeboats, steam tugs from Ramsgate and the Deal "South-end" lugger *England's Glory*.

Sixty two local boatmen shared an award of £7,000. Among them were Spears and Middleton, part owners of the lugger. Perhaps the windfall encouraged them to chance their arm - to put it mildly - in search of further rewards.

Boatmen derived much of their income from rescue and salvage work and from supplying sails, anchors and chains to ships in the Downs. The way costs were calculated and claims settled left plenty of scope for sharp practice.

In January 1867 the owners of the American ship *Kit Carson* were comprehensively fleeced. Spears and Middleton (with Baker, a pilot) took the Antwerp-bound ship to an unsafe birth in the Downs, and played only a minor and rather ineffectual part in putting things right.

Then followed grossly inflated claims for services rendered, and for the supply of replacement anchors and superfluous new sails. Local arbitration failed to protect the interests of the owner and underwriters, on whom the preposterous costs were intended to fall.

The Kit Carson (Picture: NancyDeVita/shiverickships.com).

The captain, anxious to be on his way, joined in the scam. At the subsequent enquiry only one person who had been on the *Kit Carson* was reckoned to have given honest and trustworthy evidence – a Belgian pilot.

In a parallel case involving a second American ship, the *Bazaar*, "the discovery of the truth...was rendered impossible by the determined obstinacy of W Spears to remember any circumstances happening while he was on board the ship".

But it took the case of the *Olivia* to bring Spears and Middleton down. Having persuaded the ship to anchor in the Downs they connived in – possibly caused – the parting of the anchor chain and the slipping of the cable, and persuaded the captain to falsify the log.

In August 1868 Spears, Middleton and Baker were brought to trial at the Kent Summer Assizes on eighteen counts of fraud. They were found guilty, and received six months hard labour.

The cases were extensively reported in The Times. Set against the undoubted bravery of Deal boatmen in saving life "was the habit of demanding exorbitant sums for the slightest assistance in saving property".

For the Solicitor-General it was a national disgrace: the facts of the *Olivia* case would "in great measure justify the character given by foreigners to the English coast".

The people of Deal, of course, were on the side of the boatmen. For the Mayor and Alderman Cavell, appearing at the trial as character witnesses, Spears and Middleton were honourable, upright and honest.

How was their behaviour to be squared with this glowing testimonial? In part perhaps because cheating far-distant owners and, especially, anonymous underwriters felt to them like a victimless crime.

But there was more to it than that. It was the constant complaint of boatmen at that time that, although they could be well rewarded for a successful salvage, there was no reward for saving a life.

As the author of the official report on the *Bazaar* case explained: "if boatmen save a collier and its hands, at the risk of their own lives, they are very poorly paid".

They therefore consider, he said, that when they render "little or no service to a large and valuable vessel they are to be overpaid to make up for the deficiencies in the former case".

Fair's fair, in other words.

The two boatmen in the *Olivia* case met very different ends. Poor William Middleton was one of those who drowned when the lugger *Reform* sank in 1871.

The lugger Early Morn and her crew, c. 1876.

William Spears, in contrast, lived to be 83. "The hale and hearty appearance which characterised his personality to the last was not out of harmony with the more prosperous and adventurous days with which his memory will be associated".

He left an estate worth over £1,600.

"Cheating boatman charged for rescues", published on 20 February 2019.

25.

The tragedy of the Pride of the Sea

The seaside town of Shanklin lies on the east coast of the Isle of Wight. In Victorian times Deal, Walmer and Kingsdown luggers, cruising the Channel in the hope of finding a ship in need of a pilot, often put in there for provisions.

In the early morning of Sunday 30 October 1887 a small punt was spotted washed ashore near the lifeboat station. It had belonged to a lugger which could now be seen, on her beam ends, crushed against the rocks between Shanklin and Luccombe.

The wreck of the Pride of the Sea.

Later that day a body was washed ashore. This proved to be John Moss, captain of the 18 ton Walmer pilot lugger the Pride of the Sea. Three other bodies soon followed.

The previous 24 hours had seen heavy waves and howling winds. Local boatmen concluded that the Pride of the Sea must have been creeping along the coast to seek shelter in Shanklin Bay and had struck a rock at low tide.

The local paper commented that Deal luggers "are wonderfully good sea boats and, although the waves ran high, it is not thought that she could have capsized in deep water".

John Moss, aged 53, married with six children, had a half-share in the boat. His brother William, who also lost his life along with their nephew Charles, held the other half-share.

Charles Selth also drowned. He left behind a wife and daughter. At first there was hope that 31-year old Henry Kirkaldie had escaped, perhaps having earlier been put aboard a ship as a pilot, but his body was washed ashore a week later.

The Moss brothers had only recently paid off the last mortgage taken out to buy and equip the Pride of the Sea. Times were hard: in twenty days at sea there had only been one call on their services.

Another Walmer lugger, the Cosmopolite, which had sheltered from the storm in nearby Bembridge, returned to Deal after the tragedy with nothing to show for three weeks at sea.

Thomas Adams, the sixth member of the Pride of the Sea's crew, had a miraculous escape, having boarded a ship the previous Thursday to pilot her to Dunkirk.

Taking a steamer back to Deal, he arrived on Monday to learn of the death of his friends but to the joy of his family, who had thought him lost.

"A pleasanter boat's crew never sailed than his late companions", said Adams, "and during the whole of the time he had been one of the crew he had never heard an angry or unkind or unpleasant word on board".

The lugger and equipment had been worth around £600 but were uninsured. For the owners of boats engaged in such risky work the premiums were prohibitively expensive.

Shanklin boatmen worked hard to strip the vessel and to save the hull. They later estimated that £150 - £200 worth of equipment and timber might have been salvaged, to the benefit of the victims' families.

But, allegedly, coastguard officials put a stop to this, saying that the wreck needed to be inspected. Soon afterwards heavy seas threw the lugger higher up on to the rocks – "a broken, battered, worthless skeleton" – and the chance was lost.

The wreck thrown against the rocks.

Ashore the people of Shanklin did all they could. The funeral procession and service drew large numbers of mourners. Teams of boatmen and coastguards carried the coffins, each draped with a white ensign, up the steep hill to the church of St Saviour-on-the-Cliff.

"We have often been visited by the Deal pilots", wrote the vicar of St Saviour's, "and had learned to look upon them as friends".

A public subscription for the men's families was very generously supported. A parallel appeal was launched in Deal, with a special committee formed to solicit donations.

Mourners at the memorial to the five boatmen.

Funds were also raised in both towns for a permanent memorial to the five men in the graveyard at St Saviour-on-the-Cliff.

It takes the form of a cross, made as if from weather-beaten oak, standing on rocks and with an anchor attached to the cross standing alongside.

Thomas Adams, the lone survivor, lived to be the owner of a sailing yacht, the Moss Rose, and other small craft beached just north of Deal Castle.

The Cosmopolite, the Pride of the Sea's sister ship and later famous as the very "last of the luggers", spent her final years slowly rotting on Walmer beach before being sold in the 1920s for £2.10s and broken up.

"Lugger crew deaths after rocks crash", published on 17 October 2018.

Local people mentioned in the articles

Edward Adams	40	Thomas Flitch	29
Thomas Adams	89 – 90		
Alice Allen	13	Private Goodbon	69
David Almond	50, 59	Emma Gunner	13
Thomas Bailey	77 – 80	Thomas Hayward	22
Reginald Barnes	20	Isaac Hayward	22
John Bass	81	George Head	44
Steed Bayly	45 – 60	Chris Hicks	15 – 16
Brockman Beal	61	Lewis Hill	77
Edward Blown	82	Benjamin Hulke	31 – 32
Henry Brassey	10	William Hulke	31 – 32
Thomas Brothers	28		
Vernon Brown	62	Amelia Kemp	13 – 14
Eliza Browne	7	Ann Kennett	36 – 39
Frederick Browne	6 – 8	William Kennett	36
Edward Browning	62	Henry Kirkaldie	89
William Browning	40	Edward Hugessen Knatchbull-Hugessen	9 – 12, 81
Superintendent Capps	54		
William Carterfield	34 – 35	John Iggulden	31
Thomas Cattermole	52		
Ann Cauterel	28 – 29	James Laming	17
Alderman Cavell	87	George Leith	26
Herbert Clarabut	43	William Licence	68
George Cottew	58, 71	Charles Lindsell	44 – 45
William Coulson	28	John Lobdell	29
J W Court	41 – 42	Richard Long	30
John Currey	82 – 83		
Richard Currie	59	John Mackins	67 – 68
		John Mantle	54, 56
John Dixson	31	Susannah Marsh	13 – 14
Samuel Dodsworth	59	Arthur Matthews	16
Revd Henry D'Ombrain	60	Eileen Matthews	17
Charlotte Donoghue	13	Jessie Matthews	15, 17
		John Matthews	15, 17
James Barber Edwards	18 – 19	Willie Matthews	16 – 17
Percy Edwards	59	John May	31, 33
James Elson	39	Eliza Mackenzie	62

Miss McCormick	45
George Mercer	18 – 20
Susanna Mercer	20
John Mercer	18
William Middleton	85 – 87
Billy Monckton	55 – 56
Charles Moss	88
John Moss	88 – 89
William Moss	88 – 89
Thomas Oakley	31 – 33
Samuel Olds	67
Stephen Parker	40
George Peterson	75
William Pettet	71
Bill Pierce	60
John Pittock	28 – 29, 43
William Pittock	29
Bugler Pittock	69
Steve Plews	60
Moses Potter	29
James Pratt	40
Stephen Pritchard	66
Revd Norman Radcliffe	27
George Rolfe	62
George Rose	75
Henry Rushbury	21 – 24
Charles Selth	89
Alfred Simmons	68
Thomas Sladden	52
Henry Spears	66
William Spears	85 – 87
George Tandy	53
Margo Thompson	60
Mary Thompson	15
Morris Thompson	72

William Turk	44
Peter Underwood	28 – 29
Revd Henry Venn	25 – 27
Arthur Webster	62
John Williamson	19 – 20
Henry Wood	40
William Wyborn	33

Acknowledgements

Thank you to Beth Robson, formerly of the East Kent Mercury, who edited the Mercury Memories pages over this period, and to Anita Luckett who transformed my first twenty five contributions into this book.

It is also a pleasure to thank fellow contributors, past and present, for their help and friendship: David Chamberlain, Gillian Chiverton, Judith Davies, Steve Glover, Gregory Holyoake, Pat Smith and Colin Varrall.

Many of the articles here could not have been written, by me at any rate, without access to copies of the Deal Mercury on microfilm in Deal Library and to the local history collection there.

So thank you, not for the first time, to the staff at Deal Library for their unfailing help, and also to the Deal Museum, the Sandwich Guildhall Museum, the Kent History and Library Centre, the British Library and the London Library.

And thank you, as always, to Elizabeth.